FREEDOM'S RIVER

FREEDOM'S RIVER

The African-American Contribution to Democracy

by James Steele

The African-American Experience

FRANKLIN WATTS
New York Chicago London Toronto Sydney

Frontis: *United States territory west of the Mississippi River, which was divided into slave and free lands as a result of the Missouri Compromise of 1820.*

Library of Congress Catalog Card Number: 94-61517
ISBN: 0-531-11184-9

CONTENTS

FREEDOM'S RIVER

INTRODUCTION

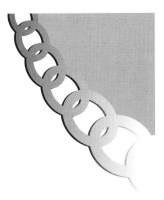

I've known rivers

I've known rivers ancient as the world and older than the flow of human blood in human veins.

My soul has grown deep like the rivers.

I bathed in the Euphrates when dawns were young.

I built my hut near the Congo and it lulled me to sleep.

I looked upon the Nile and raised the pyramids above it.

I heard the singing of the Mississippi when Abe Lincoln went down to New Orleans, and I've seen its muddy bosom turn all golden in the sunset.

I've known rivers:
Ancient, dusky rivers.

My soul has grown deep like rivers.

—*The Negro Speaks of Rivers*,
by Langston Hughes

Imagine the historic struggle that African Americans have waged for freedom and equality from 1619 to the present as a river. Imagine this river winding through time, its width changing constantly as it wends its way down mountain ranges of oppression, across plains of racial hostility, through valleys of neglect, toward its end: the liberation from discrimination and poverty.

At one point this river flows slowly but surely within well-defined banks. At another it narrows, becoming shallow and still, or suddenly it deepens into swirling rapids that rush over thunderous waterfalls, only to slow again to a drift, its forward motion barely perceptible.

Risings in this river can be likened to the role of tributaries in the great Mississippi flood of 1993. These swollen subsidiaries, powerful in their own right, emptied their surging waters at the point of confluence into the mainstream, and brought Old Man River to flood stage. The African-American freedom movement—let's call it the River of Freedom—is such a tributary. At pivotal moments in U.S. history, its surging currents widened the nation's democratic channels.

The River of Freedom not only expanded the democratic mainstream, but in crucial instances also forced the country to uphold its democratic principles. Such was the struggle against the mounting power of the slave states, in which the outcome could be only one nation, slave or free, but not slave *and* free. In this and other periods in history the African-American struggle to be free played a decisive role in preserving "government of the people, by the people, and for the people," and the constitutional system.

African Americans have inspired companion struggles of Latinos, native Americans, women, gays and lesbians, disabled people, and organized labor. The anthem of the civil rights movement, "We Shall Overcome," has become the inspiration of democratic struggles the world over.

During some periods, like a river, the African-American struggle has appeared to be placid, change imperceptible, and progress painfully slow. Every now and then, unexpectedly intense and prolonged downpours of black protest, combined with a heavy melt-off of patience, swelled the militant currents flowing in the River of

10

Freedom. The resulting pressure broke the levees of oppression that racist authorities had erected to restrict its flow. Whenever the River of Freedom overflowed the banks of proscription, nothing could hold it back.

Each upsurge—slave rebellions, militant abolitionism, the black convention movement, black Civil War soldiers, Radical Reconstruction, the alliance of the National Negro Congress and CIO union organizing drives, the civil rights revolution, or the political empowerment movement—challenged the nation to make real its promise that all people are created equal. These and countless other episodes constitute a continuum of struggle, confronting the nation with its "unfinished business."

It is said that the great flood of 1993, a revolt of the Mississippi River and its tributaries against artificial restrictions, was momentarily and massively destructive. In contrast, the historic upsurges in the African-American struggle have had enduring impact; they were massively creative revolts against a racist status quo; against violations of African Americans' dignity as individuals, as a people, as citizens of the United States; against the limitations on their right to "life, liberty, and the pursuit of happiness."

Indeed, if flooding is a river's way of changing its course, the cresting of the River of Freedom in direct mass action has been the African-American community's way of changing the course of the nation. These changes made America better, truer to its ideals, and more democratic than it would have been had slaveowners and segregationists held sway.

The reader may be more familiar with discussions of contributions of African Americans in the areas of sports, music, and lately, electoral politics, not with the development of democracy. However, the truth is that many of the cornerstones of American democracy were laid in the struggle of African Americans to make the American Dream come true not only for themselves, but for all Americans, without regard to "race, color, religion, sex, or national origin."

11

The onrushing waters of the River of Freedom forced presidents, Congress, the Supreme Court, and tens of millions of citizens to grapple with the reality that they could not say that they were in favor of democratic rights and representative government and not struggle against slavery, segregation, and disfranchisement.

African Americans, ably supported by allies in the white community and among other racial minorities, compelled Congress and the courts to uphold and the executive branch to enforce the equal protection clause, due process, and the equal administration of justice, and to expand the Constitution with new amendments detailing a more inclusive democracy. Through it all blacks have demonstrated an inexhaustible capacity to "compel unwilling authority to heed the mandate of justice."

In resisting the racism directed toward them, African Americans have proved repeatedly that, in the words of Frederick Douglass, "power concedes nothing without struggle." They have energized those who would be free "to strike the first blow for freedom," in the words of Crispus Attucks.

In the pages that follow, an attempt is made to shine a spotlight from a historical perspective on the route of the River of Freedom. The reader is given an overview of some of the bold and brilliant African Americans who navigated the most treacherous stretches of the rapids in the period from the American Revolution to the end of the civil rights movement of the 1960s. The author's goal is to acquaint young people in particular with how and why the broad currents of African-American resistance played a singularly decisive role in refining democracy in America. They may embrace this legacy and be inspired to "wade in the water" of the River of Freedom—that is, undertake to do in these times what the heroic men and women mentioned in the following pages did in theirs, many of whom were themselves youths when they accomplished great deeds.

STRIKE THE FIRST BLOW FOR FREEDOM

$\mathbf{F}$rom the darkest days of chattel slavery, African Americans have played a singular role in keeping the hope of an inclusive democracy alive. From before the American Revolution, African Americans identified with the great liberating slogans of the struggle against British domination. Thus, the ideals of revolution—Patrick Henry's "Give me liberty or give me death!" and the principles of "inalienable rights" and "all men are created equal"—inspired hope and encouraged action in slaves and free blacks alike.

Blacks saw liberation from the British as the prelude to liberty for themselves. Independence presented an opportunity, as Frederick Douglass would proclaim a half-century later, for those who would be free to strike the first blow.

So it was for Crispus Attucks on the chilly morning of March 5, 1770, in Boston, Massachusetts. Attucks, a large, strapping, forty-seven-year-old man, had declared his independence from slavery more than twenty years earlier. A slave with "an attitude," he had run away from his master. Ever since then he had been in no mood to tolerate even the thought of being deprived of his rights. Now a free man, he still had an attitude. A shipwright and seaman by trade, he had been known to knock a few heads.

Boston was certainly the proper place for independent-minded souls; it was a town rife with anti-British agitation. Scuffles with British soldiers were frequent. More than in almost any other colony, the people of Massachusetts Bay Colony—and especially the Bostonians— resented the arrogance of British authorities, who would take citizens' property, sometimes forcing them to house the king's soldiers. Taxation without representation and other abuses aroused the indignation of all segments of the population: the merchants because the imposition of tariffs thwarted their ability to compete with their British counterparts, manufacturers and artisans because the requirement to buy British-made goods inhibited the development of indigenous industry; and workers, indentured servants, and slaves because colonialism infringed on civil rights, reinforced subjugation, maintained the slave trade, and restricted individual liberty.

On that winter day, Bostonians had had enough. They were angry and were not going to take it anymore. Attucks led a group of workers in protest, shouting: "The way to get rid of these soldiers is to attack the main guard!" The British responded by opening fire. Crispus Attucks was the first to fall. Although four others were also killed in "the Boston Massacre," he, their leader, was the first martyr of the American Revolution.

The irony of his sacrifice was evident to many in the independence movement. The existence of slavery in the land of liberty would provoke controversy at the Continental Congress in the debate over the text of the Declaration of Independence. The same contradiction would plague the drafting of the Constitution, give rise to a war between the states, and cast a shadow over the nation's democratic development up to the present. As the noted historian John Hope Franklin wrote:

> . . . The significance of Attucks's death seems to lie in the dramatic connection which it

pointed out between the struggle against England and the status of Negroes in America. Here was a fugitive slave who, with his bare hands, was willing to resist England to the point of giving his life. It was a remarkable thing, the colonists reasoned, to have their fight for freedom waged by one who was not as free as they.[1]

The Boston Massacre inspired American revolutionaries to speak out against the British and against slavery often in the same breath. Abigail Adams said it is a "most iniquitous scheme . . . to fight ourselves for what we are daily robbing and plundering from those who have as good a right to freedom as we have.[2] Thomas Jefferson declared that the abolition of slavery was "the great object of desire in the colonies."[3] Thomas Paine, perhaps the most brilliant propagandist for independence, went further. In his tract *African Slavery in America*, published in 1775, he denounced the hypocrisy of the colonists; he said it was inconsistent for them to condemn the British slave trade while themselves preserving the institution of slavery in America.[4] A year later the Continental Congress passed a resolution prohibiting the importation of slaves to any of the thirteen colonies.

Despite this growing antislavery sentiment, the real test of where the anticolonial revolutionaries really stood came in the debate on Thomas Jefferson's draft of the Declaration of Independence. Jefferson, himself a slave-owner, condemned King George III for maintaining the slave trade, for preventing the colonies from restricting the importation of slaves, and for attempting to set slaves against colonists. He called this ". . . paying off former crimes committed against the *liberties* of one people, with crimes which he urges them to commit against the *lives* of another."[5]

Those who favored slavery, although Jefferson was not among them, realized that if the outright condemnation of slavery was one of the premises of declaring independence from Great Britain it would be impossible to maintain this dehumanizing system once the ties with Great Britain had been cut. In their view, Jefferson's eloquent phrase "all men are created equal" and that they "are endowed by their Creator with certain inalienable rights; among them: Life, Liberty, and the Pursuit of Happiness," was fine if it only applied to white men, but seditious if it included Africans. Threatening to withdraw their support for independence, the slaveowners demanded the deletion of all references to the abolition of slavery.

Antislavery forces compromised the nation's democractic ideals by agreeing to the preservation of undemocratic treatment of African Americans. Neither this disgraceful compromise nor the discrimination African Americans faced in attempting to take part in the war of national independence deterred them from fervently supporting the anticolonial revolution. At the start of hostilities, they were excluded from military service; however, manpower shortages and British military victories soon forced George Washington to give weapons to African Americans. Perhaps some of the colonists feared that once blacks possessed weapons they might not put them down until they had gained their own liberty as well.

African Americans fought in virtually every major battle of the war.[6] They took part in the battles of Lexington, Concord, and Bunker Hill, where Peter Salem and Salem Poor distinguished themselves as soldiers. Blacks fought at Ticondergoa, Saratoga, and Yorktown. Two African Americans, Prince Whipple and Oliver Cromwell, made the famed crossing of the Delaware River with General George Washington. Blacks suffered with their compatriots at Valley Forge and served with the Minutemen and the Green Mountain Boys. They worked behind the lines. They functioned as spies and saboteurs. They fought in the fledgling navy—Caesar Terront piloted the "Patriot" and was cited for his sterling contribution. Mark Starlin, the first African-American captain in Virginia history, staged daring raids on British ships anchored at Hampton Roads. And in a spirit of revolu-

16

tionary solidarity similar to Lafayette, a Haitian battalion called the Fontages Legion helped prevent the rout of Continental forces at the siege of Savannah.[7]

Blacks, free and slave, must have calculated that the momentum of revolution would compel an independent America to complete its mission. Many slaves did obtain their freedom during and immediately after the war. Some were freed by the British. Thousands left with British troops after the surrender of Cornwallis at Yorktown. Thousands won their freedom by virtue of their service in the Continental Army and Navy. Thousands more were "manumitted [freed]" by slaveowners earnestly committed to the democratic fervor of the times. Perhaps as many as 100,000 slaves acted on their own interpretation of the meaning of the Declaration and simply fled; some making their way to Canada, others to Florida territory, which was then under Spanish control (Spain prohibited slavery in its colonies). Countless others took refuge with the Native American tribes, or hid in the swamps, woodlands, or mountains, where they formed their own societies and staged guerilla raids on slave plantations.[8] The will to be free was evident in a thousand different ways.

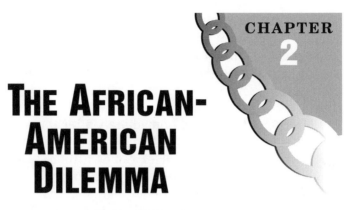

THE AFRICAN-AMERICAN DILEMMA

The Founding Fathers Didn't Really Mean "All Men Are Created Equal"

The defeat of British colonialism delivered a stunning blow to the world's supreme colonial power, and inspired a generation of movements for national independence throughout the Americas and the Caribbean. These were aimed not only at British, but also French, Spanish, and Portuguese colonialism—Haiti, victorious in 1803, Mexico in 1810, South America beginning in 1812, and Central America in 1821. The volley the American anticolonialists fired at the battle of Lexington (and Concord), Massachusetts, was "a shot heard 'round the world."

The fact that colonial power in the American colonies was not replaced with an indigenous authoritarian regime, but with a democratic republic made the American Revolution one of history's truly great revolutions. The postwar challenge was to convert the ideals of the Declaration of Independence into a coherent system of government.

The decentralized structure of the Articles of Confederation, which had been adopted during the war, was grossly inefficient. The proposal of a new centralized constitutional system, however, raised as many questions as it answered. What would a centralized system look like? How were dictatorial tendencies to be prevented? What about the rights of the states relative to a national government? What rights and responsibilities would citizens have? How strong should that government be?

Finally, would the new constitutional system be slave or free? Perhaps a majority of Americans believed that human bondage was inconsistent with the principles for which they had fought and won their independence. Many people wanted slavery to be abolished, and this was well under way in many northern colonies before the war's end.

Abolitionism

During and immediately after the war, abolitionist sentiment swept through the former colonies, especially those whose economies were not based on slave labor. Antislavery societies were formed in the North and the South. Symbolically, the very year the Constitution was adopted, 1787, Benjamin Franklin became president of the American Anti-Slavery Society, which had been founded in his hometown of Philadelphia.

A number of states prohibited slavery. Vermont abolished it in 1777. In 1780, Pennsylvania, which had acted against the slave trade during the war, prohibited the enslavement of any child born after that date. Rhode Island and Connecticut acted similarly in 1784. Massachusetts adopted a state constitution that stated "all men are born free and equal," and a short time later, the state's chief justice held that this provision abolished slavery. A parallel clause in the New Hampshire constitution was upheld on the same basis. In New York and New Jersey, powerful mercantile interests that were allied with the big slaveholders of the South blocked immediate emancipation, but measures permitting gradual emancipation were enacted.[1]

Manumission—the voluntary freeing of slaves by their

owners—assumed the proportions of a mass movement. Religious groups, particularly the Quakers and the Methodists, played prominent roles. The Quakers were instrumental in founding antislavery societies. After having resolved that "slavery is contrary to the laws of God, man, and nature, and . . . contrary to the dictates of conscience and pure religion," the Methodists pressured their members to forego slave ownership.[2]

Counterrevolution Within the Revolution

Slaveowners, and the merchants and bankers allied with them, became alarmed at the rise of abolitionism and manumission. Thus, the spread of abolitionism soon encountered a conservative backlash. From the viewpoint of slaveowners, abolition anywhere in the Union—whether immediate or gradual—threatened slavery as a system elsewhere in the Union. That, and the presence of free blacks, directly challenged the racist stereotype of inherently inferior, passive slaves on whom benevolent white masters had to bestow the virtues of "Christian civilization." Slave masters regarded free blacks, especially those active in the abolitionist movement, as having the worst kind of influence on slaves.

Meanwhile, the common folk were taking the Declaration of Independence literally and setting out to build a nation true to egalitarian principles. Antislavery and other democratic sentiments became intertwined. Slaveowners wanted to prevent any infringement on property rights, especially on the prerogatives of big landowners. Their defense of slavery put them at odds with small farmers, workers and artisans, women, abolitionists, Native Americans, and of course African Americans, slave and free.

The Profits from Slavery

The propertied elite understood that ending slavery would greatly affect their class privileges. To alter the institution of slavery was to tamper with the enormous profits unpaid slave labor generated—not only for slaveowners, but also for the merchant and traders who transported either slaves to the Americas, or tobacco, sugar, rice, and cotton grown by slaves. Manufacturers in New England or Europe, principally Britain, turned the raw materials picked by slave labor into myriad goods for domestic and foreign markets. Monied classes in the North were only partially dependent on profits from slavery, but the Southern elite was totally dependent on slavery for economic survival.

When the Constitutional Convention began its fateful deliberations in May 1787, the status of slavery was not a question that preoccupied the nation. Nonetheless, slavery was linked to the fundamental issues the proposed Constitution would have to tackle: the structure of the federal authority; the distribution of powers between the national government and the states; admission of new states; and the degree of individual liberty allotted to American citizens.

Federal authority would be divided into legislative, executive, and judicial branches. The national legislature would have two houses. Seats in the House of Representatives would be apportioned according to the number of residents in each state. The Senate would have two senators for each state, who would serve six-year terms. The Senate would be chosen by the state legislatures, not directly by the people. U.S. senators were not elected by direct popular vote until the Seventeenth Amendment was passed in 1913.

The allocation of two senators per state was a concession to the men of property who feared popular rule, especially the slaveholders. As subsequent developments would prove, this provision was a disaster for antislavery and other democratic forces. Because of their members in the U.S. Senate, the slave states could exercise a veto on national policy, whether or not the issue pertained to slavery.

The Senate quickly became the anvil upon which the

slaveholders hammered the national interest to fit their regional interests. The exaggerated political power of southern conservative senators again and again forced the national to compromise with slavery and injustice. From this position the slavocracy would drive the nation down the road to civil war.

The debate over how to determine a state's representation in the House of Representatives compelled the delegates to confront the issue of slavery. The question was whether slaves should be counted in apportioning congressional seats. The southern states wanted slaves to be counted—without slaves having the right to vote. Delegates from free states insisted that if slaves were to be counted for purposes of representation, they should have franchise rights. The slave states then threatened secession, thus forcing a partial compromise: Article I, Section 2 of the Constitution said that, in addition to whites, and excluding Native Americans not taxed, the states shall count "three-fifths of all other persons" for purposes of determining congressional representation. Other components of the compromise included Article I, Section 9, which gave U.S. citizens permission to participate in the African slave trade for an additional twenty years, until 1808, and Article IV, Section 2, which required all states to cooperate with the return to their masters of fugitive slaves.

On the question of the distribution of powers between the federal government and the states, the Constitutional Convention gave to the states all powers not delegated to the federal government. The slave aristocracy, and their segregationist descendants, would conduct the business of the South under this banner of states' rights for the next 167 years.

The slave states yielded to the fact of abolition in the North and did not seek to undo it. Instead, they made their ratification of the Constitution conditional on the right to preserve slavery in those states in which it already existed. Left open was the question of whether slavery could be expanded into states that might be admitted to the Union in the future. Concession here, as in counting the slave as three-fifths of a person, was again the price they demanded for ratification of the Union.

The Constitutional Convention was conducted in secrecy. No sessions were open to the public. There were no background briefings, press leaks, or "anonymous sources" in those days. Antislavery societies, free blacks, the abolitionist clergy, and the slaves themselves could not directly impact the debate, except through the handful of delegates who were militantly opposed to slavery. The abolitionist movement was in an unenviable position. It either had to be for or against the document as a whole when it was submitted to the states for ratification. Abolitionism at that point did not have organizational strength, nor the level of mass support, to expel the slave system from the nation.

Although fundamentally flawed in this respect, the document signaled a new era in representative government and created an enduring model of a democratic republic built on federalist principles. The Constitution would prove crucial to subsequent struggles to include Americans of African descent in the democracy it had established.

First, the Constitution replaced dispersed state power with a strong central government. A federal structure now had the authority to make and enforce the law of the land—perhaps even to abolish slavery and grant full citizenship rights to African Americans.

Second, the system of checks and balances made the accumulation of dictatorial powers by any branch of government, political party, state, or group of states practically impossible. These institutional barriers prevented the complete usurpation of federal authority by the slaveholders.

Third, each branch had its separate basis of political authority. Each branch could act independently of the others. In some circumstances, judicial interpretation by the courts might perform the role normally played by legislative action. In others congressional initiative might be used to set public policy if the executive branch refused to act, or acted against public opinion. The power of the presidency might fill the vacuum created by congressional gridlock. At one or another point in their long journey toward equality, African Americans would ally with one or another branch of government, pressuring Congress, the White House, or the Supreme Court to play a role in the expansion of democracy for people of color.

Fourth, vehicles of popular initiative were built into the structures of representative government. The exercise of the right to vote could drive elected representatives to enact public policy the people favored.

Fifth, the procedures for amending the Constitution meant that, given the right time, place, and circumstance, the unfinished business of the Constitutional Convention could be completed.

Nevertheless, in the midst of consolidating the experiment that inspired the world, the Constitutional Convention conceded the political core of the federal system to the diametrical opposite of democracy. In preserving slavery, the founders formalized an irreconcilable contradiction that would continue to haunt liberty and democracy, threatening the nation's existence more than once. The coexistence of slavery and freedom, discrimination and democracy, within the confines of representative government was a contradiction that could only grow worse with time. Seventy-five years later the nation would be compelled to wage a war against itself because of the founders' betrayal of the promise of an inclusive democracy. As during the creation of the Declaration of Independence, at the Constitutional Convention African Americans came to the brink of inclusion, but were once again excluded.

SLAVERY RISES FROM THE DEAD

By the time the Constitution was ratified in 1787, slavery had all but disappeared in the North. The economic reasons were compelling: the cold weather ruled out cultivating cotton, sugar, rice, and tobacco; and increases in European immigration provided an abundant pool of cheap wage labor. Also, the rising tide of abolitionist sentiment in the New England states produced a wave of antislavery legislation.

According to the first U.S. census conducted in 1790, 750,000 blacks lived in the United States. In the North the effects of abolitionism had been felt. Less than 4,000 of New England's 13,000 blacks were still slaves. Vermont and Massachusetts had none at all. Connecticut, with its tobacco farms, accounted for more than half the slaves in New England. Fifty thousand African Americans lived in New York, New Jersey, and Pennsylvania, but only 30 percent of them were free.[1]

The South of the 1790 census was quite different from the North. Of the 670,000 blacks living in the South as a whole, 640,000 were slaves. Although Kentucky and Tennessee had yet to be admitted to the Union, only 500 of the 15,000 blacks living in these two territories were free.[2] In total, blacks were 19 percent of the country's 4 million inhabitants.[3] However, the slave system was in deep crisis. The tobacco market was glutted, the price of slaves had fallen, and rice and indigo production was unprofitable.[4]

Slavery might very well have collapsed had not a number of economic and technological developments come together. First, the Industrial Revolution in England transformed the production of textile goods and created a seemingly insatiable demand for cotton fiber. Second, the climate in the South favored extensive cultivation of cotton. The cotton gin invented in 1793 by Eli Whitney made cotton production much more efficient. It is ironic that Whitney's invention, which would contribute so mightily to the renewal of slavery, was reportedly based on a crude model developed by a slave in Mississippi. Third, the territories of the Louisiana Purchase, and the land further west that was owned by Mexico, appeared available for the expansion of slavery.

The combination of these factors resuscitated the plantation slave-system. So long as textile manufacturers were willing to pay top prices for cotton, fabulous profits were assured. These developments cemented an alliance between Southern slaveowners and Northern merchants and financiers that had been begun in the colonial era.

Cotton production intensified the exploitation of slaves. DuBois estimates that at its peak plantation cotton production killed the average male slave within a decade or two. The male slave, overtaken by exhaustion, demoralization, corporal punishment, or incapacitating injury, could not expect to live beyond his thirties. Female slaves were used extensively in the fields as well. And once slaveowners turned to breeding to meet the demand for slave labor, the toll on female slaves and slave families was even more excruciating.

Cotton cultivation exhausted the soil at an unbelievable rate and devoured slave labor. The slaveowners had to replenish their slave supply and expand westward. By 1820 the need to expand the slave territory had become acute.

The Northwest Ordinance of 1787, drafted by Thomas Jefferson, forever forbade slavery and involuntary servitude in the Northwest Territory. (The states of Ohio, Indiana, Illinois, Michigan, Wisconsin, and parts of Minnesota would be carved out of this region.) But Congress had not declared its intentions concerning the Louisiana Purchase, which President Thomas Jefferson had acquired from France in 1803 for fifteen million dollars. The climate here favored the plantation system. Nor, in the aftermath of the Mexican War of 1846-48, did Congress define the status of the huge tract of land (eventually the states of Texas, New Mexico, Arizona, California, Nevada, Utah, and parts of Oklahoma, Colorado, and Wyoming) taken from the Republic of Mexico, although slavery had been abolished by Mexican authorities.

Westward the slaveowners pushed—into the Mississippi Valley, down into the delta country, across "Old Man River" into Texas, Kansas, and Missouri. In these vast expanses lay virgin land, rich soil, and favorable climates— ideal conditions for big plantations stocked with thousands of slaves. Some planters envisioned a slave empire that stretched all the way west to the Pacific Ocean and southward as far as Brazil. Planters thought nothing of land grabbing or fugitive-slave hunting.

The Missouri Compromise

When Congress convened in December 1819, to debate Missouri's application for statehood, one of nine (20 of the 181) members of the House of Representatives owed their election to the fact that slaves were counted for the purposes of representation but could not vote. If slaves had been left out of the count, the South's confessional delegation would have been reduced substantially. New York Senator Rufus King noted,

> . . . while 35,000 free persons are requisite to elect one representative in a state where slavery is prohibited, 25,559 free persons in Virginia

have as much power in the choice of representatives to Congress, and in the appointment of
presidential electors.[5]

The contradiction between disproportionate slaveowner congressional power on the one hand and representative government on the other came to a head in the
controversy over the condition for Missouri's admission
as a state. The numerical balance of the Senate was fairly close, with the North holding thirteen seats and the
South ten. The slaveholders were adamant. They threatened secession if Congress prohibited Missouri from permitting slavery.

The militant abolitionists, a distinct minority in the
country and the Congress, were virtually alone in giving
any thought to what perpetuation of slavery meant for
the slaves. In the debate, Representative Arthur Livermore
of New Hampshire asked, "How long will the desire for
wealth render us blind to the sin of holding both the bodies and souls of our fellow men in chains?"[6]

The abolitionists in Congress were willing to risk the
Union. New York's Senator King declared that the extension of disproportionate slave power "would be unjust and
odious." Representative Tallmadge of New York's resolution
prohibiting slavery in the Missouri territory and emancipating the slaves already there passed in the House. He
declared, "Our votes this day will determine whether the
high destinies of this region, and of these generations,
shall be fulfilled, or whether we shall defeat them by permitting slavery, with all its baleful consequences, to inher-
it the land."[7] To the threat of secession, he responded
angrily, "If dissolution of the Union must take place, let
it be so! If civil war, which gentlemen so much threaten,
must come, I can only say, let it come."[8]

Anxious to avert confrontation, the northern states
settled for a proposal put forward by Senate Henry Clay of
Kentucky. Known as the Missouri Compromise of 1820,
it admitted Missouri without an explicit restriction on

slavery. In effect, it allowed slavery. However, the compromise did bar slavery forever in all territories above Missouri's southern border, the 36°30' parallel—which was most of the Louisiana Purchase. To preserve the numerical balance between slave and free states, Maine was detached from Massachusetts and admitted as a free state.

The Missouri Compromise maintained the rough parity between slave and free states. The "irrepressible conflict" had been tabled, not resolved. Moreover, the Missouri Compromise proved that the North would retreat in the face of threats of secession.

The opposing sides collided again in 1828 when the South objected to an increase in the tariff on imported goods. South Carolina Senator John C. Calhoun, who had become the South's principal spokesperson, asserted that states had the right to nullify or disobey federal laws with which they disagreed. This time the southerners not only threatened secession, but armed action as well.

Although a slaveowner himself, President Andrew Jackson was bent on preserving the Union. In retaliation, he threatened to hang Calhoun and to use his powers as commander-in-chief to ruthlessly suppress any attempt at secession.

Armed confrontation between the slave states and the federal government appeared imminent. Henry Clay proposed another compromise: a ten-year period during which the tariff would be returned gradually to the 1816 level. The North's agreement gave the South another victory. The tariff struggle did not directly touch the question of slavery, but it did sharpen the confrontation between the conflicting interests of southern planters and northern industrialists.

The tariff controversy also brought into the open the growing power of slavery as the central concern of American politics. Thereafter, the aggressiveness of the slaveowners surfaced in practically every domestic and foreign policy issue facing the nation. More was involved than simply North versus South. Proslavery and anti-slavery alliances were being consolidated. For the next generation, these forces would clash repeatedly over the character of new states: first in relationship to the annexation of Texas, then the Mexican War, followed by the Wilmot Proviso.

Annexation of Texas

Until 1826, when it finally gained its independence, Mexico had been a colony of Spain. The Spanish readily permitted American immigration on the condition that only Catholics come, that they not bring slaves, and that they recognize Spanish sovereignty. The American immigrants and their backers had become intoxicated with seemingly endless prospects for expansion. They declared that annexation of Mexican territory was the "manifest destiny" of the United States. After agreeing to the conditions set by Spain, they proceeded to flagrantly violate every one of them.

In 1836 Americans in the territory of Texas declared their independence from Mexico and waged a war of secession, amply aided by the U.S. government. For the next nine years, Texas functioned as an allegedly independent republic. It was finally admitted to the Union in 1845, a year before the United States, operating under the banner of "manifest destiny," declared war on Mexico. It was a colossal land grab.

In the midst of the Mexican War, President James A. Polk—partly to cover up the blatant aggression—asked Congress for two million dollars to "compensate" Mexico for what would be the annexation of nearly one-half of its landmass. (Again the states of Texas, California, Arizona, New Mexico, Utah, Nevada, Colorado, and a portion of Wyoming would come from this territory.) The South wanted this vast territory carved up into slave states. Their admission to the Union would make the slavocracy dominant in the country as a whole.

The Wilmot Proviso

To the consternation of the slaveowners and expansionists, Representative David Wilmot, a Free Soil Democrat from Pennsylvania and an abolitionist, introduced an amendment to Polk's request. The Wilmot Proviso okayed this payment—some preferred to call it a bribe—provided that "as an express and fundamental condition to the acquisition . . . neither slavery nor involuntary servitude shall exist in any part of said territory, except for crime, whereof the party shall first be duly convicted."

It twice passed the House, and although southern senators filibustered it to death in the Senate, the concept embodied in the Wilmot Proviso became the eye of a gathering storm over the extension of slavery and the disproportionate power of the slaveholders.

In 1850 the nonslave states in Congress were presented a list of ultimatums by John C. Calhoun on behalf of the slave states. Slavery must be allowed in all lands seized from Mexico, every state in the Union should be obligated to capture and return fugitive slaves, and Congress must place strict prohibitions on abolitionist agitation.

The South had called not only for repeal of the Missouri Compromise, but in effect, for the abrogation of the Bill of Rights. In essence, the Southerners demanded that Congress renounce its right to legislate the conditions for the admission of new states, and suppress the right to free speech, to free assembly, and to petition the government for a redress of grievances. This was nothing less than a direct assault on democracy, particularly on the separation of powers, the system of checks and balances, and representative government.

Beginning in the heady days of the signing of the Declaration of Independence, the South had haughtily proclaimed states' rights. But now it had no problem suppressing the rights of the free states by forcing them to perpetuate an institution they had long since abolished.

Compromise of 1850

The South had raised the stakes again in the Compromise of 1850. The North acceded to yet another compromise engineered by Daniel Webster of Massachusetts and, of course, Henry Clay of Kentucky. The vaunted Compromise of 1850 consisted of five separate pieces of legislation:

- The Texas and New Mexico Act, which paid Texas the sum of ten million dollars allegedly for concessions it had made in the drawing of its borders. The bill also provided that, upon entering the Union, New Mexico itself would decide on the legality of slavery.
- The Utah Act, which allowed Utah to determine whether slavery would exist within its borders.
- Admission of California as a free state.
- The District of Columbia Act, which abolished the slave trade in the nation's capital.
- A far more stringent Fugitive Slave Act, which assigned the task of apprehending fugitive slaves to federal marshals. It also obligated the states to cooperate in the capture and return of runaways.

The biggest advantage for the South in the Compromise of 1850 was the precedent it set of allowing new states, not Congress, to decide the status of slavery. States' rights had been elevated to national policy.

This encouraged slaveowners to flood new territories seeking statehood with proslavery colonizers. Equally important, the Fugitive Slave Act dealt a severe blow to the abolitionist movement. Kidnappers now had constitutional sanction to hunt down free blacks on the allegation that they were runaways. This act forced many free blacks to move to Canada. It thus robbed the African-American community and the abolitionist movement of many of the most effective leaders and activists.

Taken as a whole, the Compromise of 1850 revoked the Missouri Compromise of 1820 and laid the foundation for overturning the Northwest Ordinance's prohibition on slavery. This alerted antislavery forces to the lengths to which the slave states were prepared to go in their grab for national power.

Proslavery forces dominated the Democratic Party, and the Democratic Party dominated the White House during the 1850s. This alliance in the Democratic Party was made up not only of slaveowners and southerners generally, but also of many western settlers and northern workers, especially new European immigrants.

The workers and settlers who voted Democratic resented the pro-business planks in the platform of the Whig Party and to some extent in the newly formed Republican Party as well. They were opposed particularly to proposals to give away public lands to railroad barons instead of making the lands available to homesteaders. They also felt threatened by calls for protective tariffs, Republican resistance to regulating railroad freight rates and its support for a national banking system that would undoubtedly fall under the control of Wall Street financiers.

The Dred Scott Decision

In 1857 a Missouri-born slave named Dred Scott brought suit in federal district court claiming that he was a free man. Years earlier, Scott had been taken by his master to live in Illinois, a free state. later his master took him to a part of the Louisiana Purchase where the Missouri Compromise prohibited slavery. When his master returned him to Missouri, Scott sued for his freedom on the grounds that residency in a free state made him a free person.

Scott's case went all the way to the Supreme Court. In a stunning setback to the movement against slavery, the court ruled that Scott was not a citizen; therefore, he could not even bring suit. Chief Justice Roger B. Taney, speaking for the court, declared that the Compromise of 1850 rendered the Missouri Compromise unconstitutional, therefore, slave masters could take their slaves anywhere they wanted, for as long as they wanted, and retain title to them. Citing the proslavery clauses of the Constitution,

Taney effectively overturned the antislavery provisions of the Northwest Ordinance. This made slavery legal throughout the nation. And, as if to pour salt into an open wound, Taney maintained that blacks "had no rights a white man was bound to respect."[9]

Slavery's Growth

The number of slaves increased rapidly after 1820. In 1790 the country had about 700,000 slaves. By 1830 there were more than two million. Thirty years later, as the nation stood on the brink of civil war, there were almost four million.

During the Constitutional Convention in the spring and summer of 1787, slavery had been concentrated in Virginia (which had the largest number), Maryland, North Carolina, South Carolina, and Georgia. Seven decades later, slavery would also dominate Florida, Alabama, Mississippi, Louisiana, Arkansas, Texas, Oklahoma, Kansas, and wide areas of Missouri.[10] Half of the total number of slaves would work on the plantations of only four states: Georgia, Alabama, Mississippi, and Louisiana.

Yet there were only 384,884 slaveowners in the entire South in 1861 when hostilities broke out. Fully three-fourths of the white population neither owned slaves nor had a direct economic interest in slavery, although a majority certainly supported its perpetuation.[11]

Slavery Expands

The geographic expansion of the slave system to new states threatened to upset the delicate balance of power that existed between slave and free states in the Senate. Although the more populous and faster growing Northern states held sway in the House of Representatives, from the beginning of the Union the North and South had almost always held the same number of Senate seats. There was an informal agreement that each time a free state was admitted, the admission of a slave state would shortly follow, or vice versa. As long as the South kept pace with the North in the Senate it could effectively veto legislation not to its liking. The admission of new states in the West held the key to the relationship of forces in the Senate, and therefore, the Congress.

The slave states were ideologically cohesive. They wielded power on the basis of a nearly complete unanimity of views on goals. The North's political power was greater, but diffuse. Senators and representatives from the North held all manner of opinions on slavery. Its unity was fractured further by intense class and regional differences. Merchants often wanted one thing, manufacturers another, and farmers still a third. Northerners ranged from militant abolitionists, passive opponents of slavery, tacit supporters of human bondage, all the way to open allies of the slavocracy.

The North was also divided by differences in party affiliation—Democrats, Whigs, Republicans, the "Know-Nothing" American party, Free Soilers, as well as the Liberty Party. Furthermore, each of these parties suffered deep ideological cleavages. The opposite situation existed in the South. The overwhelming majority of voters were Democrats, a handful were Whigs, and the Republican Party was virtually nonexistent.

The North had superior numbers in terms of states and overall population, stronger industrial capacity, abundant agricultural production, and a more highly developed transportation system and communication network. The need for a grand alliance against slavery that embraced the majority of the population was in evidence everywhere. However, without a political center and a platform that was broad enough to unite all of these forces, and that could mobilize their collective strength, such a coalition was impossible.

With the slaveowner-dominated Democratic Party already preeminent in presidential politics, the South could control the nominations to the Supreme Court and the rest of the federal judiciary. The positions southerners took in key congressional debates made the slaveowners' agenda clear: high tariffs, no tax breaks to stimulate manufacturing industry, no giveaways of public lands to homesteaders or for railroad construction, minimal spending on infrastructure development, a nationally enforced fugitive slave law, an annexationist foreign policy, suppression of antislavery agitation, legalization of the "peculiar institution" throughout the nation, and restoration of the African slave trade.

The "irrepressible conflict" between slavery and democracy reflected a clash of opposing class forces. The economic strength of slavery thwarted the extension of industrialization to the South, inviting the enmity of Northern manufacturers and investors.

Low tariffs would have been disastrous for northern industry, and thus to northern workers. The South's policy on public spending would have inhibited the development of logging and mining. It also would have had a disastrous impact on the development of a national transportation and communication system.

Conceding the best lands to planters would have disrupted the prospects of small farmers. The subsequent soil depletion typical of slavery would have destroyed the productivity of American agriculture. Slavery's expansionism collided with small farmers who also sought to settle the West.

The antidemocratic character of the slave states was already glaringly evident. Property qualifications and other aristocratic restrictions effectively disenfranchised large numbers of subsistence farmers and so-called hillbillies that the slave system marginalized. As a consequence, nonslaveholding whites were vastly underrepresented in the electorate, and practically excluded from federal, state, and local legislative office.

Now that their system was expanding at will and generating big profits, the slaveholding planters became more assertive in upholding their "way of life." The slaveholders wielding political power nationally that was disproportionate to their numbers threatened to secede from the Union, if they did not get their way on questions of tariffs, taxes, annexation, and abolition.[12]

Slavery posed an increasing danger to the democratic gains of the American people as a whole. The manumission movement in the South was stamped out; antislavery advocates were tarred and feathered and run out of the South.

The slave states demanded that free states cooperate in apprehending fugitive slaves and that antislavery agitation cease. In making these demands, the slavocracy and its defenders were assailing the principles of representative government and the freedoms guaranteed by the Bill of Rights. The slaveowners flaunted the Constitution itself, reinterpreting it at will, maintaining that the Constitutional Convention had sanctioned slavery throughout the United States.

King Cotton had undermined the tenuous quasiliberated status of free blacks in the North and the South, subjecting them to illegal search and seizure under fugitive slave statutes. The economics of slavery discouraged wage labor, which could not possibly compete with slave labor.

The incredible economic and political power of the slave plantation aristocrats allowed them to dictate to the rest of the South.[13] Now they thirsted for control of the federal government. But, should this prove unattainable, the slave barons were prepared to tear the republic asunder and impose a secessionist slave state on half of the country.

Slavery's innate expansionism and aggressiveness put it on an irreversible collision course with wage labor, small farmers, northern industrialists, the abolition movement, and the mass of slaves. The growing power of the slaveholders stood in the way of the fuller democratic development of the nation. The backwardness of the slave economy was an obstacle to the emergence of a capitalist national economy. Sooner or later, the nation would have to decide: either be slave *or* free; but not slave *and* free.

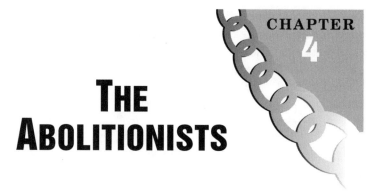

THE
ABOLITIONISTS

The contribution of African Americans to their own liberation from slavery was as enormous as it was varied. First, the ranks of the abolitionist movement were infused with a growing contingent of courageous free African Americans who, as skilled orators and organizers, helped to mobilize mass opposition to slavery.

Second, the black convention movement transformed the resistance of free blacks into a national movement. Third, in addition to explicit political writings, African Americans also created a body of antislavery literature. For example, by the time of the Civil War, America's notable men and women of letters included the following African Americans: William Wells Brown, whose *The Escape or a Leap to Freedom*, made him America's first African-American playwright and *Clotel: or the President's Daughter*, published in 1853, made him the first African-American novelist; historian William C. Nell; Martin R. Delaney, who is known as the father of black nationalism; Samuel Cornish and John Russwurm, editors of the first African-American newspaper, *Freedom's Journal*; and, of course, Frederick Douglass, who published and edited *The North Star*, later renamed *Frederick Douglass' Paper*.

Fourth, the emergence of an independent, multidenominational, black American church provided the foundation upon which an independent national freedom movement was built. The Free African Society founded by Richard Allen and Absalom Jones in Philadelphia in 1787, the year the Constitution was drafted, was the precursor of the first black church: the African Methodist Church. By the 1820s it was the leading organization among black Methodists.[1] In fact, it was Richard Allen who as leader of the African Methodist Episcopal Church launched the black convention movement in 1830 to help galvinize black clergy, laymen, and secular forces to intensify the struggle against slavery.[2]

An independent Baptist church took root among free African Americans in the early 1800s in response to the discrimination they experienced in white Baptist denominations. By 1850 the number of black Baptists had reached 150,000, making it the largest African-American denomination of the time.

The independent African-American church, as well as religious groups that allowed blacks into their congregations or engaged heavily in missionary work among the slaves, were often sources of antislavery activity. This was particularly true of the Quakers. C. Eric Lincoln and Lawrence Mamiya, in their chronicle of the black church in the African American experience, observe, "Among quasi-free blacks, mutual aid societies and churches were among the first institutions created by black people.[3] In the 1840s white Baptists split over the issues of slavery.

The slavemasters used religion to suppress African cultures and to instill submissiveness, but religion, once blacks began to "Africanize" it, or inject their own unique cultural content into it, also became a vehicle for resistance. In fact, in the aftermath of the revolts of Denmark Vesey and Nat Turner, black religious activity was ruthlessly suppressed by the slaveowners.[4]

Black spirituals became a code for sending messages from plantation to plantation, sometimes alerting slaves that the Underground Railroad was coming that particular night. Imagine, for example, the "other" meaning of:

> *Swing low, sweet Chariot*
> *Coming for' to carry me home*
> *Looked over Jordan*
> *And what did I see*
> *Coming for' to carry me home*

And,

> *Go down, Moses,*
> *'Way down in Egypt land,*
> *Tell ole Pharaoh*
> *To let my people go.*

Generally slaves resisted in two ways: they ran away or resorted to day-to-day resistance—sabotaged crops, destroyed machinery, staged slowdowns and work stoppages, burned plantations, conducted insurrections. Free blacks supplemented slave resistance by penning militant journalism on the evils of slavery.

The growing African-American contribution enabled the abolitionist movement to spread during the 1840s, and especially in the wake of the Compromise of 1850. By the middle of the 1850s, antislavery sentiment and abolitionist activity swept New England, the states of the Northwest Territory, and wide swaths of the Louisiana Purchase.

The willingness of African Americans to strike the first blow for freedom, whether in the abolitionist movement or later on the battlefields of the Civil War, demonstrated to their fellow citizens that as individuals and as a people they were the equal of any other group. Their persistent struggle was forcing the issue: one nation—slave or free, but not slave and free; a democracy or a slavocracy, but not both.

The Underground Railroad

Harriet Tubman was the most famous conductor on the Underground Railroad. The mere mention of her name must have sent shivers of rage up and down the spine of slavemaster and overseer alike. Frail and reasonably well along in years, Tubman repeatedly entered the South— nineteen times in all—to lead runaway slaves to the North and on to Canada. She reportedly brought more than 300 slaves to freedom.

So effective and inspiring was she that slaveholders offered $40,000 for her capture, dead or alive.[5] She never was caught, and she never lost a passenger. Nor did she tolerate cowardice or retreat. She was known to have pulled her pistol more than once and offered a bullet to the faint of heart.[6]

There was John Fairfield. Born into a Virginia slave-holding family, Fairfield could not bring himself to commit the "sins of his fathers." He would have nothing to do with slavery, choosing instead to move to the North. Actually, he had to move North after helping a slave friend escape to Canada. Thus began his career as an Underground Railroad conductor. He would take descriptions of friends and family of runaways and head South, at times posing as a slaveowner, slave trader, overseer, peddler, and once as an undertaker. He would locate his passengers and bring them North. On one occasion he brought twenty-eight slaves to freedom in a staged funeral procession.[7]

Levi Coffin was an Indiana-based Quaker. Coffin's farm was a kind of Grand Central Station of the Underground Railroad. He also coordinated a network of Quaker spies and operatives who assisted the Underground Railroad and the abolitionist movement. Known as the "president of the Underground Railroad," he is said to have helped as many as 3,000 slaves make their way to freedom.

The Underground Railroad was like a long, drawn-out strike in which the ingredient of the slave system—

unpaid labor—withdrew from production. Governor Quitman of Mississippi complained that between 1810 and 1850 nearly 100,000 slaves, valued at thirty million dollars, rode its rails to freedom. Slaveowners were obsessed by what could be called the "chance-chance" syndrome: slaves ran away if they got the chance; or they would do the slaveowners serious harm if they got the chance.

The Fugitive Slave Act of 1850 was a direct response to the effectiveness of the Underground Railroad. As a result of the Act, the slaveowners turned the South into an armed camp, imposed thought control, virtually suspended the Bill of Rights for whites, and enacted Slave Codes. Nevertheless, they could not contain slave resistance, rebellion, and runaways.

The daring and ingenious acts of rescue and escape on the part of black conductors and passengers contradicted the carefully constructed thesis of docile, contented slaves who preferred servitude to freedom. Reports about these bold ventures inflamed abolitionist passions in the North and, quiet as it was kept, in some quarters of the South as well.

Slave Insurrections

The most drastic form of resistance was the insurrection. Historian Herbert Aptheker says that more than 250 slave revolts occurred between the colonial era and the Civil War. Three revolts—those of Gabriel Prosser, Denmark Vesey, and Nat Turner—were significant for their scale, scope of conspiracy, and psychological impact on the slave aristocracy.

On April 30, 1800, Gabriel Prosser launched an uprising of more than one thousand slaves. He had intended to lay siege to Richmond, Virginia, and overthrow the slave regime. Betrayed from within, Prosser's forces were routed. Upon capture he declared:

> I have nothing more to offer than what General Washington would have to offer, had he

been taken by the British officers and put to trial by them. I have ventured my life in endeavoring to obtain the liberty of my countryment, and am a willing sacrifice to their cause; and I beg, as a favour, that I may be immediately led to execution. I know that you have predetermined to shed my blood, why then all this mockery of a trial?[8]

In June 1822, Denmark Vesey, a slave who had succeeded in buying his own freedom, engineered a plot to take control of Charleston, South Carolina, drive out the slaveowners, and establish an independent republic of emancipated slaves, or failing that, exit en masse to Haiti. Vesey had carefully paved the way for his revolt with four or five years of relentless, quiet agitation among slaves and free blacks. He would quote Toussaint L'Overture, the leader of Haitian independence, or recite Old Testament passages about the Israelites being delivered out of bondage in Egypt (precisely why the slaveowners banned teaching slaves to read).[9] He carefully and patiently assembled an underground organization to carry out insurrection, recruiting an estimated 9,000 slaves from the Charleston area.[10]

Vesey's plot was also betrayed. Forewarned, South Carolina's slave regime staged a preemptive strike against the insurrectionists. Denmark Vesey and his coconspirators were arrested and hanged. What shocked the slaveowners most was not the fact of a conspiracy, but Vesey's daring, the brilliance of his plan, and the sophistication of his organization.

Nat Turner's rebellion is undoubtedly the most famous of all slave rebellions. It began on August 21, 1831, also in the state of Virginia. Turner's goal was to do away with the slave system by doing away with the slaveowners. Unlike Prosser and Vesey, Nat Turner's rebellion got off the ground. But as it unfolded, one of the worst rainstorms in Virginia's history hit. With his forces left in disarray by the storm, Turner's rebellion was defeated. More than one hundred slaves were killed in pitched battles with white vigilantes, the Virginia militia, and federal troops, but not before dozens of slaveowners were killed and scores of plantations razed to the ground.

Thirteen slaves and three free blacks in the leadership were sent to the gallows as punishment. Turner, who was not captured until the end of October, met the same fate.[11] Hysteria swept the high society of the planter aristocracy. Slaveowners and overseers feared another Nat Turner might lurk in the heart and mind of every slave. The relatively small number of slave revolts suggests that the slaves themselves must have sensed that a successful insurrection was impossible. Yet Prosser, Vesey, and Turner gave testimony to the slaves' boundless determination to be free and their willingness to use any means necessary to achieve liberation.

The slave rebellion, the Underground Railroad, the runaways who formed "maroon" colonies in the mountains or swamps from which guerrilla warfare against the slave plantation system was waged, or who formed alliances with the Native Americans to resist encroachment on their lands, the plantation saboteurs, the many expressions of day-to-day resistance, slaves' clever ridicule of "ways of the white folks," the spirituals—all were hallmarks of the growing desperation and intensification of resistance. These were also the signs that the slaveholders, for all their arrogance and vaunted power, ruled a system nearing its end. Slavery's death would turn out to be as violent for the country as it was in life for the slave.

ABRAHAM LINCOLN AND FREDERICK DOUGLASS

Point and Counterpoint in the Struggle Against Slavery

Benjamin Quarles writes that, "Free-born or slave-born, the Negroes who became active abolitionists were generally the most able men in the group, the cream of the crop."[1] No leader, black or white, was more brilliant, more skilled in the articulation of democratic principles, or more dedicated and able in practical politics than a runaway slave named Frederick Douglass. Self-taught, uncompromising, thoughtful, and diligent, Douglass was the strategic visionary of the abolitionist movement. More than any other leader of the nineteenth century, more than Garrison or Phillips, Lincoln or Grant, Douglass understood the historic imperative of the times:

> . . . abolition or destruction. You must abolish slavery or abandon the Union.[2]

Douglass's ability to give leadership to the nation at critical junctures distinguished him from other antislavery

leaders: Lincoln, the Radical Republicans, the abolitionists, and the Free Soilers. His capacity to convey the "lesson of the hour" sustained him through a career of public
service leadership that would span fifty years. In the
1850s, when the irrepressible conflict came to a head,
Douglass shifted his support to the fledgling Republican
Party, even though most abolitionists were congregated
in the small and somewhat influential Liberty Party,
which had the politically correct line of immediate and
total abolition, but no mass following nor prospects of
building one. The less-focused Republican Party, founded
in 1854, which was much maligned by abolitionists because
it opposed only the expansion of slavery, did have such a
prospect.

Douglass alone among abolitionist leaders appreciated the significance of the Republican Party and the direction in which it was developing. It had come into being in
opposition to the Kansas-Nebraska Bill, another in a long
line of infamous compromises with slavery. This bill con-
tained the doctrine of "squatter sovereignty" that allowed
the settlers living in a territory to decide the status of
slavery instead of Congress.

The legislation's passage in 1854 precipitated bitter
armed conflict between proslavery and abolitionist forces
in the Kansas and Nebraska territories. The slaveholders
conceded Nebraska's entry into the Union as a free state,
but they wanted Kansas to come in as a slave state. The
slaveholders sent thousands of colonizers into this sparse-
ly populated area to ensure a proslavery outcome. The
proslavery forces physically drove out the Free Soilers,
who were fairly numerous and well organized. Civil war
followed; hence, the term "bleeding Kansas."[3]

The Republican Party was founded in the midst of
this turmoil. National outrage had been simmering in
response to the Fugitive Slave Act and the Kansas-
Nebraska Bill, and later, the Dred Scott decision.[4] The
antislavery forces flocked to the newly formed Republican
Party, which had a broad-based platform that attracted
Whigs, including Lincoln, who were fed up with their

party's fence-sitting on the question of slavery; antislavery Democrats repulsed by slaveowner domination of their party; abolitionists who favored political action; Free Soilers who were doing battle with proslavery elements in the territories; assorted activists for women's rights, labor unions, temperance, prison reform, utopian socialism; and business interests that wanted to promote the normal development of capitalism in the South.

Within a year of its founding, 15 U.S. senators and 117 members of the House of Representatives affiliated with the Republican Party. The 1856 Republican ticket, headed by the well-known abolitionist General John C. Fremont, finished second in a three-way race, receiving more than 1.3 million popular votes, carrying 11 states, and winning 114 electoral votes. James Buchanan, the Democratic nominee, won by 174 electoral votes.[5]

As Douglas understood, the Republican Party was on its way to becoming the primary vehicle for an antislavery coalition. He also knew that the self-interests of diverse sections of the nonslave states were linked indissolubly to the abolition of slavery, whether they favored abolition or not.[6] " . . . Free Soilism is lame, halt and blind," he declared, "while it battles against the spread of slavery, and admits its right to exist anywhere. If it has the right to exist, it has a right to grow and spread. The slaveholder has the best of the argument the very moment the legality and constitutionality of slavery is conceded."[7]

Therefore, Douglass emphasized that

> . . . The only way to put an end to the aggressions of slavery, is to put an end to slavery itself. While the system of slavery exists, it must, from its very nature, be aggressive. The safety of liberty requires the complete extinction of its opposite; and since the U.S. Constitution was established to secure the blessing of liberty, there is, therefore, a high constitutional, as well as moral obligation, resting upon the American people to abolish slavery.[8]

Douglass also argued that emancipation would be incomplete unless the exslaves were granted full citizenship rights, especially the right to vote. To do otherwise would be to repeat the sins of omission of the Continental Congress and the Constitutional Convention. Even before the Civil War began he had already formulated the essential tasks of postwar reconstruction.

Douglass often pointed out that what is morally right is not always politically possible. Therefore abolitionists should strive to achieve that which was possible. To those who accused him of inconsistency, he replied that all that "antislavery consistency" required was that abolitionists should deliver the sharpest blow possible against slavery at a given moment.[9]

He called on abolitionists to support the Republican ticket as they would any measure, no matter how limited, that was capable of gaining broad public support and went in the direction of ending slavery.[10] After the 1856 election, he argued that the Republican Party was "now the great embodiment of whatever political opposition to the pretensions and demands of slavery is now in the field."[11] A Republican victory in the 1860 presidential election "must and will be hailed as an antislavery triumph"[12] if for no other reason than this is how slaveholders would see a Republican administration. Douglass felt that the struggle would force Republican constituencies that had started out opposing only the expansion of slavery eventually to oppose the existence of slavery everywhere. "We have turned Whigs and Democrats into Republicans," he insisted, "and we can turn Republicans into Abolitionists."[13]

This task would turn out to be more difficult than perhaps Douglass had imagined. Lincoln, his inner circle, and the bulk of his supporters were clear about preserving the Union, but vague and halting in doing what was necessary to accomplish this. The slave states made up their minds for them. South Carolina greeted Lincoln's election by seceding from the Union in December of 1860. The following February, Florida, Georgia, Alabama, Mississippi,

Louisiana, and Texas joined it in setting up the Confederate States of America.

Then, in the early morning hours of April 12, 1861, South Carolina's secessionist supporters fired on Fort Sumter, the federal garrison in Charleston's harbor. The Civil War had begun. On April 15, Lincoln called up 75,000 troops to retake the forts and other properties the rebellious states had seized from the Union. Two days later, Virginia seceded, shortly followed by Arkansas, Tennessee, and North Carolina. Only timely military action by Lincoln prevented Maryland, Kentucky, and Missouri from leaving.[14]

Even in the face of thirteen states in rebellion over the preservation of slavery, the Lincoln administration remained adamant that the war would not be waged on the basis of abolition. The reasons for this paralysis of policy were complex. First, Lincoln was unwilling to move outside of the national mood and in the early months of the war there was not a national consensus on emancipation. Second, emancipation raised the question of citizenship rights for the ex-slaves, and at that point the influence of white supremacy was too strong for most whites to conceive of blacks as free and equal citizens. Third, a fairly substantial stratum of the North's population had a financial and commercial stake in slavery. Fourth, proslavery sentiment was strong among Union army officers. Lincoln knew it would be hard to fight the war on an antislavery basis when his troops were led by proslavery generals. Fifth, many Northern Democrats, former Whigs, and conservative Republican businessmen cited the daunting human and material costs of the war to urge "peace at any cost."

Expanding Democracy

An important deterring factor may have been the prospect of the broad democratization of economic and political life. To liberate the slaves and grant them citizenship rights would have elevated the status of poor whites in the North and the South. But up to that point property qualifica-

49

tions and other procedures excluded large numbers of whites from voting. Senators were chosen by state legislatures, which were dominated by wealthy merchants, manufacturers, and farmers. Only in the midst of war, with the South absent, was Congress able to pass the Homestead Act of 1862, making public lands west of the Mississippi available free to families that settled on them. It also passed the companion Land Grant Act, also in 1862, which financed agricultural education from the sale of public land. This measure laid the foundation for state university systems.

The fact that the absence of slaveowners in Congress created a political balance conducive to passing populist legislation drove home the relationship between the struggle for democracy and the war against secession. The war against slavery was in fact a war for democratization of the country. The more consciously it would be waged as such, the more far-reaching its democratic potential. To conduct it on an explicit abolitionist basis would likely engender a wave of radical democratic transformations and the possibility of a postwar democratic movement based on an alliance of former slaves and poor whites.

Powerful bankers and businessmen, whose support Lincoln needed to underwrite the war's financing and to maintain war production, wanted to free the South from the grip of the slaveholders so it would be free for investment and industrialization. If the Civil War became a war of liberation, a chain of events might be set loose that neither they nor Lincoln could control.

Lincoln feared that the consensus needed to conduct the war might be broken. For the first year of the Civil War, visionary leadership was lacking in the White House, the Congress, the Union army, and the Republican Party. The North was unable to mobilize its vastly superior numbers and resources. Nor could it exploit the South's greatest weakness: its war effort depended on the labor of four million black slaves.

Lincoln had won the 1860 Republican presidential

nomination because he occupied the great middle in northern public opinion. He articulated the broadest consensus on slavery: that it should remain alive in the states where it already existed, but must not be allowed to expand a single inch further. Lincoln feared to venture beyond this position.

As brilliant and incisive as Lincoln's leadership sometimes was, his initial policies were ineffective in limiting secession or in winning the Civil War. It would take unfavorable events on the battlefield to convince Lincoln that emancipation was necessary to defeat the Confederacy.

Fortunately for the nation, in Frederick Douglass it had a brilliant guide who functioned as the point and counterpoint not only to Lincoln, but to the abolitionist movement and other antislavery forces as well.

The noted historian Philip S. Foner writes: "From the very beginning, Douglass perceived clearly that the war was a struggle to complete the historic task left uncompleted by the first American Revolution, which had failed to root out the cancer of slavery from the body of America, that it would mean the emancipation of the Negro people and the liberation of the North from slaveholding domination."[15]

Douglass immediately pinpointed the essential task: "The Negro is the key of the situation—the pivot upon which the whole rebellion turns."[16] He called for the immediate and universal emancipation of the slaves, enlisting them en masse into the Union army, and assigning them to combat duty as quickly as possible. He argued that these steps were indispensable to winning the war. The first would establish that the war was about slavery, not states' rights. The second would deprive the South of the labor that supplied its troops and sustained its economy. The third would destroy the myth of black inferiority and contentment, dealing a powerful psychological blow to the Confederate leaders and soldiers. It would also encourage slave insurrections and day-to-day resistance.

Combined, these three measures would give the North its moral mission and mold its diverse antislavery constituencies into a united fighting alliance against slavery. By clarifying the war's character, the Union would be able to mobilize public opinion in other countries, particularly Britain and France. This in turn would preclude British recognition of the Confederacy, and thus prevent the world's most powerful economy from giving material aid, maintaining commercial ties, or extending diplomatic support to the slavocracy.

At first Lincoln rejected this advice, afraid of sending the border states into the arms of the Confederacy and converting the ambivalence of Northern bankers and merchants into active opposition. Lincoln also legitimately worried that emancipation would provoke the proslavery elements in the military. Some of his leading commanders, including General George McClellan, already spent more time and energy capturing and returning the slaves, who by the tens of thousands were flocking to Union lines, than fighting the Confederates.

Moreover, Lincoln held fast to the illusion that the secessionists could be persuaded to return to the Union via another compromise: gradual emancipation. To this end he supported a bill that would compensate states that agreed to free their slaves by the year 1900! Clearly he did not want to endanger a possible reconciliation with the South by emancipating and then arming the slaves. Nor had Lincoln given up on colonization. In fact, he sent emissaries to the Dominican Republic and to Central America to check into the feasibility of establishing black colonies.

Oddly enough, for all of his hesitation and reluctance, Lincoln was clearly influenced by Frederick Douglass's argumentation. The two leaders—Lincoln of the nation, Douglass of its conscience—met several times during the conflict, corresponded periodically, maintained regular contact through intermediaries, and regarded each other as personal friends. This, however, did not prevent Lincoln from continuing with his strategy, nor Douglass from criticizing him for this, sometimes sharply.

AMERICA'S WAR OF EMANCIPATION FROM ITSELF

The South had preceded the attack on Fort Sumter with a proposal to extend the line demarcating slave and free states westward from the orignial Missouri Compromise to the Pacific Ocean. Territories to the north would be free, to the south, slave. The secessionists must have known that Lincoln neither would nor could accept such a proposition. Perhaps they made it to prevent pro-Union elements in the South from reaching a compromise with the new president.

Lincoln's initial policy was to contain slavery and save the Union. He had been sworn to "preserve, protect, and defend" the Constitution. If this could be accomplished by allowing slavery to exist in the south, he was prepared to so; but destruction of the Union was entirely different. On this he stood firm. Yet this was a defensive strategy, and an offensive one was required. Saving the Union necessitated invading the South and ruthlessly suppressing the rebellion.

General George McClellan was the equivalent of today's Chairman of the Joint Chiefs of Staff. He was pro-Union, but also proslavery, and thus vigorously supported Lincoln's containment strategy. McClellan led the way in the capture and return of fugitive slaves to their confederate owners even as the war was in full swing. Battle had to be forced on McClellan. At Bull Run his forces were crushed in a tepid attempt to take Richmond, Virginia, the initial Confederate capital.

In August 1862, General John C. Fremont, who was with General Ulysses S. Grant's command, established martial law in Missouri. He issued an edict that freed the slaves of slaveowners in rebellion against the Union. Lincoln revoked this order.[1] He only halfheartedly let stay General Benjamin Franklin Butler's order declaring all property and resources used against the Union "contraband" of war. Since slaves were property this was a backdoor way of admitting slaves in Union-held territory into the North's war effort.[2]

The Union's prospects looked bleak in the first two years of the war, until General Ulysses S. Grant successfully opened a second front in the western territories. He knocked out the Confederate forces in Tennessee, then took control of the Mississippi River after defeating rebel forces in the Battle of Vicksburg in July 1863. Soon Union forces under his command opened up "Old Man River" all the way to New Orleans, with General Butler and naval Captain David Farragut leading the way. These victories split the Confederacy geographically for the duration of the war.[3]

Victory in the west was not enough to win the war. For that the Union army would have to cut out the heart of Dixie, which meant defeating the Confederate armed forces on their home turf. This task required more troops, larger resources, and greater sacrifice. A string of embarrassing, costly defeats in 1862 and 1863 at Antietam, Fredericksburg, and Chancellorsville undermined support for the war effort in the North. Recruitment was down. Public support waned, with many asking why whites should fight against slavery if blacks were kept out of the fighting. The North's war mobilization lacked focus; it had no rallying cry, except "Save the Union." Lincoln would not move without a new consensus.

Douglass urged abolitionists to mobilize public opinion in favor of abolition, emancipation, and democratization. He devoted all his energies to this task, campaigning over the length and breadth of the North, day and night, for emancipation. Everywhere he explained the importance of arming African Americans, free and freed. His strenuous efforts made a big difference, especially among working people. Abolitionists everywhere stepped up their agitation. Wendell Phillips said it all:

> Abraham Lincoln may not wish it; he cannot prevent it; the nation may not will it, but the nation cannot prevent it. I do not care what men want or wish; the negro is the pebble in the cog-wheel, and the machine cannot go on until you get him out.

In effect, an alliance between the broad abolitionist movement, the Radical Republicans in Congress, Free Soilers, industrialists, and the African-American community came into being. This tilted the balance of forces in the North in favor of conducting the war as a war of liberation. The power of this new consensus was augmented by a dramatic increase in slave resistance. An exodus from the plantations to Union lines occurred. Sabotage, spying, and insurrections became more frequent. Although not yet fully free, slaves transformed themselves from passive to active participants in this great conflict.

On March 31, 1862, President Lincoln signed legislation prohibiting Union armed forces from returning fugitive slaves. In April, Congress passed, and Lincoln signed, a bill that abolished slavery in the District of Columbia. On June 19, he signed a bill abolishing slavery in the territories. Less than a month later Congress gave the President the discretionary power to utilize African-American troops. On July 17, Congress enacted a measure freeing slaves who fled disloyal masters.[4]

Yet on the fundamental question of complete and universal emancipation the administration continued to vacillate. The longer this situation lasted, the more an antislavery outcome was in doubt. The South had been able to gain the upper hand in a number of battles, despite the Union's superiority in manpower and war production, for one reason and one reason alone: slave labor.

The Lincoln administration's approach was not working, and the President knew it. Lincoln himself would say, "Things had gone from bad to worse, until I felt that we had reached the end of our rope on the plan of operations we had been pursuing: that we had about played our last card." He would later remark, "I claim not to have controlled events, but confess plainly that events have controlled me." Push had indeed come to shove. As Douglass had predicted, Lincoln was up to the task. On September 22, 1862, President Abraham Lincoln announced:

> On the First day of January, in the year of our Lord one thousand, eighteen hundred and sixty-three, all persons held as slaves within any State or any designated part of a state, the people whereof shall then be in rebellion against the United States, shall be then, henceforth, and forever free.[5]

Then came New Year's Eve. Public vigils were held throughout the North, surreptitiously throughout the South. A few minutes before midnight, as the seconds ticked relentlessly toward 1863, the word came that African Americans had waited 244 years to hear:

> And by virtue of the power and for the purpose aforesaid, I do order and declare that all persons held as slaves within said designated States, and parts of States, are, and henceforward shall be free; and that the Executive government of the United States, including the military and naval authorities thereof, will recognize and maintain the freedom of said persons.[6]

At that moment the war was transformed. From that point on it would be conducted as an abolitionist war. The second American Revolution was now in process.

When slaves learned of Lincoln's proclamation, they often went on a general strike. They downed their tools and fled to Union lines—sometimes leaving behind plantations aflame. Soon the Confederacy faced a labor supply crisis. Confederate authorities did everything possible to prevent the "good news" from reaching the slaves. It was withheld in Texas and parts of several other states until the following June—hence, the "Juneteenth" celebrations of the Emancipation Proclamation in those areas.

Lincoln was quite deliberate when he defined emancipation as a war measure. Freed slaves in large numbers enlisted in the Union army and navy. For most of the war they received half the pay of white soldiers. They were subjected to brutal treatment as prisoners of war, and often summarily executed. More than 300 black prisoners of war would be slaughtered at the Fort Pillow Massacre. In spite of it all, African-American soldiers and sailors acquitted themselves brilliantly. Secretary of War Edwin Stanton, in a letter to Lincoln, recognized their valor. "They have proved themselves among the bravest of the brave, performing deeds of daring and shedding their blood with a heroism unsurpassed by soldiers of any other race."[7]

African Americans formed their own military units. There was the Crispus Attucks Guard of Albany, Ohio; the Hannibal Guards of Pittsburgh; and similar squads in New York, Philadelphia, and Boston.[8] More than 185,000 African Americans—nearly 10 percent of the total number of enlistees—fought in the Union army, and 29,000 fought in the Union navy. Of these, 93,000 came from the South. Thousands of African-American women were active in the auxiliary services. Black Americans fought in 410 military engagements, including 39 major battles.[9] They were on the crew of the *Monitor*. They were decisive in the Battle of New Orleans. Nearly a fourth of black enlistees perished in combat. On one day alone, September 19, 1864, in the battle to take New Market Heights outside the approaches to Richmond, twelve African Americans would win the Congressional Medal of Honor; 543 would give the "last full measure of devotion."[10] The all-black Twenty-fifth Army Corps was among the Union divisions that chased Robert E. Lee's routed troops to Appomattox Courthouse, where his surrender ended the war.[11]

Frederick Douglass and other black abolitionists played a signal role in recruiting blacks, slave and free. Two of Douglass's sons fought with the famous all-African-American Fifty-fourth Massachusetts Regiment which was the subject of the movie *Glory*. More than 200,000 black men and women worked in Union army camps as mechanics, teamsters, nurses, cooks, maintainence workers, and common laborers. Free blacks also formed aid societies to assist the emancipated slaves and helped to set up schools for the ex-slaves.

The most extraordinary of all Union spies was an African-American woman—none other than Harriet Tubman, the celebrated conductor of the Underground Railroad. Lerone Bennett writes that she organized slave intelligence networks behind enemy lines in South Carolina and other states. She led scouting parties, conducted guerrilla raids, and may have been the first and only woman to actually lead U.S. troops in battle. It was a daring incursion of 300 black soldiers that destroyed millions of dollars of stockpiled goods and carried off 800 slaves, without losing a single soldier.[12]

Frederick Douglass's work reflected the great issues at stake in the Civil War. He was constantly on the move: meeting with the President, lobbying Congress, consulting with Radical Republicans, mobilizing abolitionists, barnstorming the country, visiting the troops, rallying slaves to the Union cause. In the midst of these intense activities, Douglass again became the counterpoint to Lincoln in anticipating postwar problems of consolidating the gains that were being won on the battlefield. Douglass was the first to note the urgency of immediately granting the ballot to former slaves. Recognizing that many whites believed that blacks were too ignorant to exercise voting rights, he nonetheless proposed a strategic alliance between the North and millions of enfranchised African Americans in the South.

Lincoln also worried about the difficulties that lay ahead. One of the most widely acclaimed speeches in American history is his address on November 19, 1863, at the dedication of a national cemetery at Gettysburg, Pennsylvania, site of one of the bloodiest battles of the war. Taking less than ten minutes to deliver, Lincoln's Gettysburg Address acknowledged that the war had given the nation "a new birth of freedom." Yet there was still "unfinished business," although those who had fought there had nobly advanced it. They had given their lives so that the nation might live. "It is for us, the living, rather, to be dedicated here to the unfinished work which they who fought here have thus far so nobly advanced." He then spoke not only of the need to "bind up the wounds of war," but also of "the great task remaining before us."[13]

The Gettysburg Address revealed that the President now fully understood the implications of abolition. In context, the "great task remaining" could have only meant postwar reconstruction and the incorporation of the freed blacks into the democratic processes. He now spoke of "a new birth of freedom" in obvious reference to the Emancipation Proclamation. Hence, he became preoccupied with the practical problems connected with suddenly gaining four million new citizens. He established several departments to administer to the needs of former slaves. They were eventually subsumed under the Bureau for Refugees, Freedmen, and Abandoned Lands, or Freedmen's Bureau. Lincoln also supported a limited franchise for freed blacks. Thus, he would ask the governor of Louisiana's reconstructed state government "whether some of the colored people may not be let in [to the elective franchise] as, for instance, the very intelligent, and especially those who have fought gallantly in our ranks."[14]

Integrating the ex-slaves into the nation's emerging political economy would be one of the most formidable postwar challenges. Franklin says, "The problem of Reconstruction was essentially the problem of the emergence of a nation moving toward greater economic and political democracy."[15] The most critical component of this was rebuilding the war-devastated South on the basis of free labor.

The Civil War radically transformed the country's economics, as well as its politics. In the North, the war had accelerated industrial and agricultural production. The war had had the opposite effect on the South. The plantation economy that had dominated the region since colonial times lay in ruins.

Moreover, the war changed the nature of the federal government, which emerged from the conflict as the nation's largest employer. The Homestead Act and the Land Grant Act, the development of a true national currency, and the creation of a genuinely national banking system greatly expanded the federal government's powers. Before the war most government functions were handled at the local level. Afterward, however, the federal government played a determining role in agriculture, education, infrastructure improvement, and finance. The federal government would have to extend the same authority to the South, where little of even local government existed, and whatever law and order prevailed was maintained by the Union army.

Northern triumph cleared the way for wage labor, the Bill of Rights, and federal authority, from Maryland and Virginia to Kentucky and Tennessee, from the Carolinas and Florida to Louisiana and Texas. At least in the formal sense, the nation finally had been made whole.

THE STRUGGLE OVER RECONSTRUCTION

Postwar reconstruction would pass through several stages. The first is called Presidential Reconstruction (1864–66) because it was carried out under the near-exclusive authority of presidents Lincoln and Johnson. Presidential Reconstruction commenced with the Emancipation Proclamation and lasted until 1866, when President Johnson's allies were crushed in the midterm congressional elections.

The second stage, known as Congressional Reconstruction (1866–68), began once Congress overrode President Andrew Johnson and initiated its own Reconstruction program. This phase passed rather quickly to Radical Reconstruction as Congress began taking sharper and more far-reaching measures in response to the planter-inspired counterrevolution. This third phase commenced with the Fortieth Congress in 1868 and coincided more or less with the first term of President Ulysses S. Grant.

The Death of Lincoln
Within a month of the Gettysburg Address, Congress began debating a constitutional amendment that would prohibit slavery throughout the United States and its territories. At Lincoln's insistence, this proposal was includ-

ed in the Republican Party's 1864 presidential platform. On the last day of January 1865, with two-thirds majorities in each house concurring, the Thirteenth Amendment prohibiting slavery was adopted. The Republican president and the Republican-controlled Congress planned to enact legislation guaranteeing that the war had not been fought in vain. Enactment of a series of strictly defined, but nonetheless sweeping, laws was virtually assured.

Then, barely a month after his second inauguration Lincoln visited Ford Theatre on the evening of April 14, 1865. John Wilkes Booth, a fanatical proslavery conspirator, fired a shot into the back of Lincoln's head. The Great Emancipator was dead by the next morning.

Thus began April's sad and peculiar standing in American history, evoking events both tragic and triumphant. The secessionists had unleashed the Civil War in April. The Union had won the war in the month of April. Abraham Lincoln, elected to head a national government of Reconstruction that would "bind up the nation's wound," was assassinated in mid-April, a fate Dr. Martin Luther King, who stood at the head of a historic Second Reconstruction, would share ten days earlier, one hundred and three years later.

Presidential Reconstruction:
Johnson Sides with Counterrevolution

Within six months of assuming the presidency, Vice-President Andrew Johnson's complicity with an increasingly aggressive drive to restore the planter class to power in the defeated South was fully revealed. With the new president's help it looked as though the ex-Confederates, having lost the war, were going to win the peace. Johnson issued amnesty for rebels who took an oath of loyalty to the Union—that is, they simply had to *say* they were now loyal.

Soon thereafter, the President took it upon himself to grant pardons to former Confederate political and military leaders. Some he appointed as governors of the defeated states. He restored the suffrage rights to most of those who possessed the vote before the war, while denying the ballot to the former slaves. He also required the Confederate states to hold conventions, which were then mandated to draft and adopt state constitutions that were consistent with the U.S. Constitution. But Johnson's insistence that these state conventions establish a "republican form of government" was no more than a smokescreen for his connivance with forces that were just as intent on imposing undemocratic regimes based on underpaid black labor as they were when they seceded from the Union.

During the summer and fall of 1865, President Johnson ordered the return of confiscated land to planters he had pardoned. He began removing Freedmen's Bureau officials who were disliked by southern whites, and he spoke openly against granting the franchise to blacks. He favored "a white man's government," and at one point said "White men alone must manage the South."[1] By 1866 white supremacists were in full control of the state governments. This was evident in the composition of the delegations the Deep South sent to Congress for the 1866–67 session. They included the vice-president of the Confederacy, six Confederate cabinet officers, four Confederate generals, five Confederate colonels, and fifty-eight members of the Confederate Congress.

Although Congress refused to seats these delegates, the fact that they were elected spoke volumes about the support of the South's white voting-age population for Confederate leaders. There were other ominous developments as well: the adoption of Black Codes, Johnson's veto of the Civil Rights Act of 1866, his veto of the reauthorization of the Freedmen's Bureau. If to the victors go the spoils, Congress would have to make it so.

Meanwhile, General Carl Schurz, who had been sent on tour of the South by President Johnson, reported that "The emancipation of the slave is submitted to only in so far as chattel slavery in the old form could not be kept up. But although the freedman is no longer considered the property of the individual master, he is considered the slave of society."[2] Reconstruction would have to be fought for on two fronts: in Washington between the Johnson Administration and an increasingly radicalized Congress, and on the ground in the South between the freed African Americans and their allies, the many in North and the few that there were in the South, on the one side, and the resurgent planters and their fellow travelers, on the other.

The Black Codes

In rapid succession, one legislature after another in the southern states enacted Black Codes, which served the same functions as the infamous "slave codes." These laws amounted to a new form of slavery. The codes were an attempt to restrict the ex-slaves to plantation labor. Benjamin F. Flanders, a Radical Republican, was right; the state legislatures recognized by President Johnson spent "Their whole thought and time . . . plans for getting things back as near to slavery as possible."[3]

In Mississippi, for example, each January all blacks were required to have written proof that they had employment for the coming year. Those without it, or who left their jobs before the contract expired, had to repay the wages already earned and were subject to arrest by any white person. Vagrancy or spending one's wages inappropriately was punished by fines and involuntary labor.

Throughout 1865 and early 1866, almost all of the states restored by presidential Reconstruction passed laws that barred blacks from equal access to the courts, from full participation in the labor market, and from renting or owning land.

Florida enacted a statute that made a crime of disobedience, impudence, and disrespect shown by blacks to their employer. Louisiana and Texas passed laws obligating not only a black worker, but also all members of his family. Virginia's state legislature outlawed collective action for higher pay on the part of blacks.

Abraham Lincoln,
photographed by
Matthew Brady

Frederick Douglass,
abolitionist leader,
journalist, and
statesman

A woodcut dated 1868 is entitled *Protecting Negroes From White Backlash.* The Union army remained in the South during the Reconstruction period to safeguard the new freedoms of the ex-slaves.

Facing page: A rare photo of a black regiment shows the Provost Guard of the 107th Colored Infantry, at Fort Corcoran, one of the defenses of Washington, D.C. By the end of the Civil War, 185,000 black men had enlisted in the Union army, 85 percent of those eligible to fight.

A Currier & Ives print of African-American congressmen during Reconstruction. (Left to right) Senator Hiram R. Revels, Mississippi; Representatives Benjamin S. Turner, Alabama; Robert C. DeLarge, South Carolina; Josiah T. Walls, Florida; Jefferson H. Long, Georgia; Joseph H. Rainey and Robert Brown Elliott, South Carolina.

Facing page, bottom:
A celebration in 1888 in Richmond, Virginia, of Emancipation Day, the commemoration of the signing of the Emancipation Proclamation.

Miss Julia Hayden, a seventeen-year-old African-American schoolteacher, was murdered by the White Man's League in Tennessee in the years after emancipation.

Booker T. Washington

W.E.B. DuBois

In January 1939 black sharecroppers traveled in a caravan along Missouri highways to bring attention to their economic needs. Here the sharecroppers load up their wagons, since they were ordered by the highway patrol to return to their homes.

Workers in the kitchen of a dining car on a Streamliner train. The union of railway workers, who were primarily black, was organized by A. Philip Randolph.

During the Great Depression, Harlem's unemployed lined up
to receive food distributed by the New York City police.

At an AFL-CIO meeting on December 5, 1955: (left to right) George Meany, head of the steelworkers union; A. Philip Randolph and Willard S. Townsend, African-American vice presidents of the AFL-CIO; and Walter Reuther, president of the United Auto Workers.

An integrated group of Freedom Riders sit in the "white only"
waiting room of the bus station in Montgomery, Alabama,
May 28, 1961.

Three CORE Freedom Riders sit on the grass in front of their bus that had been attacked and burned by a mob of whites in Anniston, Alabama, May 14, 1961.

In 1963 civil rights and labor leaders met with President John F. Kennedy to discuss progress toward integration. Left to right in the front row: Whitney Young of the National Urban League; the Reverend Martin Luther King, Jr., of the Southern Christian Leadership Conference; Rabbi Joachim Prinz, chairman of the American Jewish Council; A. Philip Randolph, vice president of the AFL-CIO and founder of the railway porters union; President Kennedy; and Walter Reuther, president of the United Auto Workers.

Facing page:
An estimated 2,000 African Americans march on the Birmingham, Alabama, jail on May 5, 1963.

President Lyndon B. Johnson signs the 1964 Civil Rights Bill into law and presents the pens with which he signed the historic document to leaders gathered around his desk. Directly behind LBJ are Dr. Martin Luther King, Jr., and Whitney Young of the National Urban League. At the extreme right is Speaker of the House John McCormack and directly behind him is Mayor John Lindsay of New York.

❖ ❖ ❖ ❖ ❖ ❖

Facing page: Voting rights are honored at long last in a federal registration office in Greenwood, Mississippi. On August 10, 1965, Louis Searson, a federal voter registrar, fills out a form for a prospective black voter as dozens of others wait in line.

The great grandson of Dred Scott, John Madison, points
out to his family the unmarked grave of his ancestor in
Calvary Cemetery, St. Louis.

Most of these "crimes" carried heavy penalties. Blacks who violated them could be whipped in public, pilloried, or have their labor sold to an employer for a period of time. Thus began notorious sharecropper system under which peonage and prison labor gangs were substituted for slavery. Presidential Reconstruction had not brought democracy to the South, but greater tyranny.

African Americans Demand the Franchise

A political and economic foundation for democracy in the South had to be laid on the basis of free labor and universal suffrage rights. Four million African Americans who had never known an independent existence had to be transformed into a new class of wage laborers and small farmers.

This worried Frederick Douglass greatly. He had studied the defeat of the 1848 democratic revolutions in Europe and was painfully aware of the dangers of a post–Civil War parallel. "Thoughts of this kind," he warned abolitionists, "tell me that there was never a time when Anti-Slavery work was more needed then right now."[4] He demanded that the federal government crush slave power forever. He saw the "immediate, complete, and universal enfranchisement of the colored people of the whole country" as the most effective, and perhaps only, counterbalance to the restoration of the power of the former slaveowners.

The former slaveowners could regain control of the state governments only if blacks were deprived of the right to vote and serve in elective office. With the franchise, however, freed African Americans would have the political power to prevent their economic reenslavement by the planter class. Without suffrage rights and the power to make public policy, they would be vulnerable to resurgent plantation power and pervasive white resentment. The ex-slaves must have the right to vote, and the federal government must enforce the right.

Opposition to Presidential Reconstruction Grows

Northern opposition to Andrew Johnson's approach to Reconstruction and to the Black Codes undid his presidency and brought Presidential Reconstruction to an end. Northern industrialists and investors realized that a southern-dominated Democratic Party would favor policies that strengthened the hand of the South's landed aristocracy.

Settlers and small farmers in the West readily saw that restored planter power also threatened implementation of the Homestead Act, which had given them land. Experience had taught them that the planters would take the best land, driving the farmers to the fringes of the economy. For this reason many whites in the hill country and mountain regions of the South during the Civil War had harbored pro-Union views and hated secession, which they termed "a rich man's war."

Radical Reconstruction

These divergent forces—Radical Republicans, abolitionists, reformers, industrialists and investors, small farmers, and African Americans—would support a radical program in the South that would grant political power to freed slaves and a stable, independent, economic existence for the former slaves.

This program required dismantling the plantation system. However, this could be achieved only by taking away the land of the big slaveholders and putting it in the public domain or redistributing it to land-hungry blacks and whites. While the Confiscation Acts passed during the war had established a precedent for this, Thaddeus Stevens proposed going much further. He wanted Congress to expropriate the holdings of the Confederacy's largest landowners as a war indemnity to pay off the South's war debts, as well as to compensate the Union for its war costs. Then the federal government or Congress would award forty acres to ex-slaves and their families, not so much as a gift as partial reparation for generations of unpaid labor.

Stevens wanted to sell what remained of these holdings to poorer whites at a reasonable price. In this way, he believed, the federal government could create and economically empower a new class of free farmers, black and white. "This must be done," he argued, "even though it drives the nobility into exile. If they go, all the better. It is easier and more beneficial to exile seventy thousand proud, bloated and defiant rebels than to expatriate four million laborers, native to the soil and loyal to the Government."[5] He insisted that,

> . . . reformation *must* be effected; the foundation of their institutions, political, municipal and social, *must* be broken up and *repaid* or all our blood and treasure have spent in vain.[6]

Stevens's proposal was too radical for most Radical Republicans and received little support—even from Frederick Douglass. But history would sustain the validity of his claims. Without completing a democratic revolution, the South would never have either republican or representative institutions. The mass of poor whites would never advance above the upper reaches of poverty, and there would be no such thing as emancipated African Americans. Moreover, the democratic conditions that existed in the North would be endangered if an unreconstructed South with its outmoded economic power relationships essentially intact was permitted to rejoin the Union.

For the most part, poor whites did not support Radical Reconstruction. The influence of racism led them to side with the very rich whites who deprived them of land and liberty. The irony is that, of the available alternatives, only Reconstruction would have brought economic well-being and political participation to poor whites of town and country.

John Hope Franklin, the dean of African-American historians, stresses that Reconstruction was neither a regional nor racial issue, but a national one that gave rise to a hard-fought, high-stakes battle over its nature and scope in the Congress, between the Congress and the White House, at the ballot box, and in the states. The analysis of Stevens and particularly Frederick Douglass provided a framework in which Congress, the Radical Republicans, and for a while the country, aggressively undertook to reconstruct the South on a democratic basis.

Douglass responded to resurgent planter power by more fully elaborating a concept of the democracy he sought for his people. "Peace between races," he said, "is not to be secured by degrading one race and exalting another, by giving power to one race and withholding it from the another, but by maintaining a state of equal justice between all classes."[7] Equal justice, equality before the law, and equal protection and inclusion in a multicultural democracy were pivotal notions that would find their way into the language and spirit of the Fourteenth and Fifteenth amendments, as well as the Civil Rights acts of 1866, 1868, and 1875. They would rise again a generation later in the philosophy of the W.E.B. DuBois–led Niagara Movement, and nearly a century later in Thurgood Marshall's brief in the *Brown* decision and Martin Luther King's "I Have A Dream" speech.

Douglass also insisted on the principle of federal enforcement. He not only rejected states' rights, but promulgated a thesis of a uniform republic with a multiracial democracy. For him, the goal was:

> . . . to establish in the South one law, one government, one administration of justice, one condition to the exercise of the elective franchise, for men of all races and colors alike.[8]

Taken together, Stevens's proposal on confiscation and redistribution and Douglass's concept of multiracial democracy based on equality before the law constituted a genuinely radical program of action. It would have aligned the South economically and politically with the North and brought to life the old abolitionist slogan of "free soil, free speech, free labor, and free men and women."

Unfinished Business

There was still the matter of liquidating the doctrine of the *Dred Scott* decision, which held that "the black man had no rights the white man was bound to respect." Still another constitutional amendment would be necessary.

In the absence of African-American suffrage, the secessionist states were free to restore themselves without rehabilitating themselves.

RADICAL RECONSTRUCTION

Democracy in Dixie

Although African Americans fought for democracy during the period of Reconstruction as zealously as they fought for freedom on the battlefields of the Civil War, the outcome of this political contest was beyond their control. W.E.B. DuBois remarked in his classic study, *Black Reconstruction*, that:

> The attempt to make black men American citizens was in a certain sense all a failure, but a splendid failure. It did not fail where it was expected to fail. It was *Athanaius contra mundum*, with back to the wall, outnumbered ten to one, with all the wealth and opportunity, and all the world against him. And only in his hands and heart the consciousness of a great and just cause.[1]

Role of the Radical Republicans

The grand alliance against slavery not only emerged from the Civil War victorious, but also intact. If anything, the unity of antislavery forces appeared to have been strengthened. The Thirty-ninth Congress had passed the Civil

Rights Act of 1866 over President Andrew Johnson's veto, then ratified the Fourteenth Amendment granting full citizenship to African Americans.

In 1866 northern voters, horrified by reports of the brutality of the Black Codes and the rising tide of political terrorism against the ex-slaves, and repulsed by President Johnson' appeasement of the former Confederates, thoroughly repudiated his allies in the midterm congressional election. In the Fortieth Congress, Republicans, who ranged in political views from moderate to radical, held a 143 to 49 majority over the Democrats in the House and a 42 to 11 majority in the Senate. The 1866 congressional election put an end to the presidential phase of reconstruction.

The combination of Radical Republicans in Congress and black resistance throughout the South, enabled the nation's democratic forces to take the offensive against Presidential Reconstruction and resurgent planter power. Following Douglass's lead, the democratic movement demanded immediate voting rights for blacks and harsh punishment for the leaders of the defeated Confederacy.

Pennsylvania's Thaddeus Stevens, unquestionably the most militant of the abolitionists in the House of Representatives, and Charles Sumner of Massachusetts, who brought a long and distinguished history of abolitionism with him to the Senate, were Douglass's ideological soulmates. On Stevens' initiative, in 1866 the Congress created the Joint Committee on Reconstruction. It quickly became the vehicle through which Congress wrested control of Reconstruction policy from President Johnson. The Committee of Fifteen, as it was called, not only checked Johnson's authority and countermanded his pro-planter executive orders, but also introduced legislation launching Congressional Reconstruction.

The majority of the members of Congress were not Radical Republicans. It is more accurate to say that within a broad Republican consensus, the left wing or Radical Republicans held sway over Reconstruction policy. They had a much clearer idea of what should be done and how to do it. Their political clout was augmented by their alliance with mass democratic forces in society—the abolitionists, the black convention movement, social reformers, and a sector of northern business interests.

Legislative Framework for Radical Reconstruction

Led by Thaddeus Stevens and Charles Sumner, Radical Republicans pushed for enactment of measures that laid the legislative foundation for Radical Reconstruction. This constructed a legal framework for completing the business left over from the Declaration of Independence and the Constitutional Convention. In short order, the Fortieth Congress followed up on the Civil Rights Act of 1866, which had been passed by the previous Congress, by enacting the Reconstruction Acts and the Enforcement Acts. It also ratified the Fifteenth Amendment.

The Reconstruction Acts were approved in February, March, and July of 1867, each over President Johnson's veto. Except for Tennessee, which was permitted to remain in the Union (it had defied Johnson by endorsing the Fourteenth Amendment), the first Reconstruction Act revoked Johnson's restoration of the states that had been in rebellion. It also rescinded his general amnesty to leaders of the Confederacy. The second Reconstruction Act divided the ten remaining secessionist states into five military districts, each administered by the Union army. In effect, Congress imposed martial law on the South. It also empowered the federal government to deal summarily with violations of the Reconstruction Acts.

The third Reconstruction Act mandated that in order to rejoin the Union the unreconstructed states had to hold constitutional conventions, the delegates to which were to be elected on the basis of universal male suffrage and without regard to race. The new state constitutions were obliged to guarantee African-American voting rights. Finally, the states that had been in rebellion could not be restored to the Union until they ratified the Fourteenth Amendment.

The 1868 presidential election furnished the Republicans with compelling evidence of the importance of ensuring that African Americans had the right to vote. Even though Ulysses S. Grant, the Republican nominee, won the electoral college by a landslide, he had taken the popular vote by a margin of just over 300,000 ballots. He had overwhelming support from 450,000 black voters, while not winning a single southern state.

These results underscored the Republican Party's predicament: it could not hold on to national power without winning in the South. But blacks were the only southerners likely to cast their ballots in large numbers for the GOP. Once African Americans had the franchise, given that 90 percent of the nation's 4.5 million blacks lived in the South, the Republicans could win in the South and prevent the conservative southern-dominated Democratic Party from regaining a hold on the House and especially the Senate. At the start of Reconstruction there were over 700,000 registered black voters, nearly equal the number of whites who were eligible to vote in the states that had not been readmitted to the Union. Republican hopes of consolidating control on national power rested on the enfranchisement of African Americans.

The broad coalition of forces that favored a democratic Reconstruction policy was also alarmed by the direction the Supreme Court, still dominated by southerners and conservatives, had taken. For example, in *Ex parte Milligan*, a case that was unrelated to Reconstruction, the court called the constitutionality of the state conventions mandated by the Reconstruction Act into question. In another decision, *Cummings* v. *Missouri*, it held that martial law and the Freedmen's Bureau courts were unconstitutional. The court majority was clearly inviting a challenge to the Civil Rights Act of 1866 and the Reconstruction Acts in order to create a pretext for defeating Radical Reconstruction on constitutional grounds.

The Radical Republicans in Congress knew they had to act. Otherwise the Supreme Court would tie the federal government's hands while white supremacists spread their political terrorism against the ex-slaves to the whole of the South. The Republicans in Congress responded by adopting the Fourteenth and Fifteenth amendments. The Fourteenth Amendment, ratified on July 28, 1868, conferred citizenship on all persons born or naturalized in the United States without regard "to any previous condition of slavery or involuntary servitude." Striking a blow at the Black Codes and lynch law, it forbade the U.S. government or any of the states from infringing on the civil rights of citizens "without due process of law."

With this amendment, Congress added the missing "two-fifths" to make the status of African Americans in civil society whole. They were finally African *Americans*. In addition, the Fourteenth Amendment authorized Congress to reduce the congressional delegations of states that violated its provisions. By affirming that citizens had rights that the government could not override, the Fourteenth Amendment enhanced the civil rights of all Americans.

Without "due process," states now could not infringe on the liberties granted to citizens under the Bill of Rights. States had a constitutional obligation to respect and protect free speech, a free press, the right to protest, freedom of religion, the right to bear arms, trial by impartial jury, and to prohibit cruel and unusual punishment, as well as unreasonable search and seizure. Moreover, states could not discriminate against African Americans or naturalized citizens.

Finally, in authorizing Congress to pass legislation essential to the implementation of its provisions, the Fourteenth Amendment established the principle of federal enforcement of civil rights. The Amendment also increased the independence of the federal courts and expanded their powers to protect civil rights.

The Fifteenth Amendment, which was ratified on March 30, 1870, prohibited federal, state, and local government from imposing property, educational, "character," or any other restrictions on the right to vote designed to disfranchise African Americans. It said, "the right of citizens of the United States to vote shall not be denied or abridged by the United States or by any State on account of race, color, or previous condition of servitude."

Under the enabling legislation the Fifteenth Amendment authorized, Congress empowered the President to appoint election supervisors who could bring federal suits in cases of election fraud or voter intimidation. The 1871 Enforcement Act made schemes to deprive citizens of their right to vote, hold office, or serve on juries punishable under federal statutes. The Ku Klux Klan Act gave the President the power to suspend the writ of *habeas corpus* and declare martial law whenever a state proved unwilling or unable to protect the civil rights of African Americans.

As significant as these legislative measures were, however, neither the Republican Party nor the federal government took the steps necessary to safeguard the long-range interests of the ex-slaves. The situation required something along the lines of Stevens's proposal to confiscate and redistribute the holdings of the wealthiest former slaveowners, and Douglass's enfranchisement and empowerment proposals. However fleeting Reconstruction turned out to be, it did succeed for a time in bringing an unprecedented measure of democracy to the South.

African Americans' Concept of Democracy

The ex-slaves associated their emancipation with the great egalitarian ideas of the eighteenth century. Thus, the slave codes had forbade teaching slaves to read in the hopes of preventing them from reading the same revolutionary works that Franklin, Jefferson, and Paine read, or that matter, from reading Franklin, Jefferson, and Paine. The Black Convention movement provided a framework in which African American notions of freedom, equality, and democracy underwent continuous elaboration. After emancipation, former slaves took on names like Liberty,

Freedom, Freeman, or Franklin, Jefferson, and, of course, Lincoln. They demanded as well that whites address them as "mister" or "missus."

Former slaves regarded economic freedom as the right to own land. Without land, they reasoned, they could be reenslaved in new forms. Union army officers and Freedmen's Bureau officials reported that former slaves typically defined freedom as independence from white control, and democracy as individual and collective autonomy—the right to act under their own volition.

It is not surprising that General Sherman's Special Field Order #15, issued in January 1865, would hold extraordinary appeal. Under it, Sherman confiscated a wide swatch of the coastal low country of South Carolina that extended south from Charleston to the Sea Islands for the exclusive settlement of former slaves and their families. He had the confiscated land parceled out to ex-slave families in forty-acre units. The order also provided for loaning or selling mules to the new landowners—hence the slogan "forty acres and a mule."

Throughout the South former slaves believed that with the franchise they would be able to elect candidates of their choice, actively participate in legislative bodies, and in this way safeguard their economic freedom. Political education and political mobilization quickly became one of the main features of postwar black life, North and South. As one might expect, African Americans nationwide identified strongly with the Republican Party. They were also very active in nonpartisan organizations like the Union League, which conducted voter registration and education campaigns, and agitated for the right to vote, as well as for federal intervention to protect the civil rights, labor conditions, and land ownership rights of freed African Americans.

African-American clergy played a central role in the emerging black politics. More than 100 African-American ministers would be elected to seats in the Reconstruction state legislatures. The black church encouraged the holding of mass meetings, rallies, citizenship classes, and public discussions of freedom. More than any other institution, the African-American church may have been the greatest beneficiary of emancipated conditions. It not only grew rapidly, but also quickly consolidated its independent status. Black fraternal, benevolent, and mutual-aid societies blossomed as well.

The Freedmen's Bureau and federal troops helped facilitate the political activities of the former slaves. The Black Convention Movement flourished in this environment. From the immediate postwar years until the defeat of Reconstruction two decades later, state and local black conventions were held regularly throughout the South. Many of the future leaders of the Reconstruction state governments learned political philosophy, the in's and out's of the legislative process, techniques of political debate, and parliamentary procedure in the convention movement. For example, from the fifty-two delegates who attended the South Carolina state convention in November 1865 came four members of Congress, thirteen state legislators, and twelve constitutional convention delegates.

Former slaves also regarded freedom as an opportunity to reunite their families and establish stable community institutions. It was not uncommon for ex-slaves to take to the road in search of children and spouses.

Reconstruction-Era Black Politics

African Americans were eager to practice the democracy they preached in the bastion of oligarchy and authoritarianism. But was the rest of the country? Once again, W.E.B. DuBois was on the mark when he observed "With perplexed and laggard steps, the United States government followed in the footsteps of the black slave."[2] And thus did Congress, between the winter of 1867 and the summer of 1875, pass a sweep of legislation that for the first time defined the meaning of citizenship, detailed the outer reaches of republican democracy, gave the federal government ultimate responsiblity for civil rights enforcement, projected a broad program of social justice, and undertook the nation's first and in some ways still unsurpassed affirmative action measures.

"For a brief period," DuBois would also say, "for the seven mystic years that stretched between Johnson's 'Swing round the Circle' to the Panic of 1873, the majority of thinking Americans of the North believed in the equal manhood of Negroes. They acted accordingly with a thoroughness and clean-cut decision that no age which does not share that faith can in the slightest comprehend."[3]

Thus came to pass one of the most tumultuous, yet inspiring periods in the history of any country. In the midst of the stultifying cotton culture of Dixie's planter aristocracy, its auction blocks closed and auctioneers silenced, would arise, phoenix-like, a people long "'buked and scorned," who made a leap through centuries of slavery to emancipation, citizenship, and freedom in the space of a handful of months and years.

White supremacist propagandists, among them many of America's most lauded historians and sociologists, complained of "Negro domination." It was an odd charge coming from academicians known to sing praises of "robber barons," land swindlers, anti-Indian mercenaries, and national administrations rife with greed and graft. There was no such thing as black domination of the Reconstruction governments. Only in South Carolina did African Americans comprise a majority of the state constitutional convention delegates. And, again only in South Carolina were they a majority of the Reconstruction state legislature.

In fact, given their numbers, blacks were underrepresented at the constitutional conventions, and in local, state, and federal government. As a rule, blacks did not engage in racial bloc voting even in the jurisdictions in which they heavily outnumbered white voters.

The virtual absence of separatist or nationalist sentiment was one of the remarkable attributes of the political behavior of freed blacks. While they were unreserved in asserting their legitimate feelings of racial pride over what they were accomplishing, politically they emphasized "all"— not "them" or "us." As far as they were concerned, they were integral to "government of the people, by the people, and for the people." The resolution of the 1865 black state convention in Alabama echoed this sentiment:

> We claim exactly *the same rights, privileges and immunities as are enjoyed by white men—* we ask nothing more and will be content with nothing less (emphasis in the original— JS).[4]

This perspective explains why African Americans were not attracted to emigration. Neither African colonization nor separatist schemes enjoyed mass support. Martin R. Delaney, the "father of black nationalism," who was a Republican organizer in South Carolina during Reconstruction, noted that it was "dangerous to go into the country and speak of color in any manner whatever, without meeting with an angry rejoinder, 'we don't want to hear that; we are all one color now.'"[5]

Clearly, freed blacks thought about politics and public policy in the universal terms of what would be called "multicultural democracy" today. They sought policies that would meet common needs, and thus valued multiracial consensus and coalition. This was evident in the elections that took place in the fall of 1867 to choose delegates to the state constitutional conventions. This political posture was also reflected in the state constitutional conventions held in 1867 and 1868, as well as the elections during the winter and spring of 1868 that ratified the new constitutions and chose the first Reconstruction governments.

African-American Political Power Comes to Dixie

As legislators, executive branch officials, and voters, African Americans sought to create a society free of racial

79

distinctions in the administration of justice, fully committed to equal opportunity, and where the right to vote and hold office belonged to all. Historian Lerone Bennett, Jr., points out that "black leaders projected a political posture which envisioned the destruction of the plantation system, the bulldozing of the color-caste systems and vastly expanded social welfare programs which anticipated the New Deal."[6]

On the whole, the performance of the governments they helped to lead was well above the norm for the times. The policies they pursued and the programs they implemented reflected African Americans' aspirations to attain what slavery had denied them: suffrage rights, land, education, personal security, stable families, access to culture. Black elected officials in particular fought to replace an authoritarian South with one that respected the Bill of Rights. South Carolina's Reconstruction constitution proclaimed:

> Distinction on account of race or color, in any case whatever, shall be prohibited, and all classes of citizens shall enjoy equally all common, public, legal and political privileges.[7]

Generally blacks favored an activist model of government. Nearly all of the state Reconstruction constitutions established a woman's right to divorce, to enter into binding contracts, and to own property independent of her spouse. They also abolished property qualifications for voting. On the initiative of black elected officials or because of pressure from black constituents, the Reconstruction governments significantly expanded the public sector, creating the South's first public school systems, hospitals, orphanages, mental health facilities, and penitentiaries. Reconstruction governments also pioneered the use of public works to equalize wages and provide employment for workers who had been excluded from certain jobs because of their race or national origin. This policy not only helped blacks enter skilled jobs, but in Mississippi helped Chinese workers to do so as well.

By the late 1860s and early 1870s a large number of blacks held powerful local offices like county supervisor, tax collector, and education commissioner, especially in states where candidates for these positions were elected, not appointed. Hundreds of African Americans served as city policemen and rural constables. They comprised half of the police force in Montgomery, Alabama, and Vicksburg, Mississippi, and more than a quarter of the police departments of New Orleans, Louisiana; Mobile, Alabama; and Petersburg, Virginia.

The political empowerment of African Americans also empowered large numbers of poor whites. The elimination of property and literacy qualifications for voting enlarged the number of poor whites who could now vote. Many of these whites turned around and voted against the very Reconstruction governments that gave them the ballot. This is especially tragic given the fact that it was usually black legislators who introduced and most eagerly supported debt relief legislation, which was crucial to white small farmers in saving their land.

Black elected officials made a significant difference in the quality of the lives of freed blacks and poor whites. African Americans pioneered measures, the first in southern history, that provided tax-supported compulsory public education. The Reconstruction governments surpassed many northern states in the breadth of social justice they achieved, such as founding first state mental health institutions as well as schools for the disabled. Clearly, whites benefited as much from these and other measures as did African Americans.

Radical Reconstruction threatened the plantation system with its lazy landed-aristocracy, and also white supremacy, its ideological pillar. If blacks, less than a decade removed from slavery, were capable of running state governments, ably participating in the deliberations of Congress, and governing local jurisdictions as competently as whites—often more so—it would be difficult to argue that African Americans were an inferior people. And if blacks and whites proved themselves able to govern together for the common good, what would be the point of returning to the rule of a few whites—any few, whether wealthy southern landlords or rich northern industrialists?

Lerone Bennett observes that, "Not corruption but honesty, not ignorance but brillance horrified racists during the Reconstrcution era. If there was anything Southern whites feared more than bad black government, it was good black government. If there was anything they feared more than an ignorant black politician, it was a brillant one."[8] The expansion of democracy on the basis of the economic and political empowerment of freed blacks undermined the privileged status of white elites. However, the empowerment of blacks reduced the power of only some whites—those who had wielded power selfishly, lavishly, and ruthlessly generation after generation.

African-American political empowerment worried wealthy industrialists who coveted the South's resources and its cheap labor. The Reconstruction governments that had already checked the power of white supremacy might do the same to burgeoning big business. As these monied interests became dominant in the Republican Party, it became quite different from the party Frederick Douglass and the Radicals envisioned. Reconstruction, with its radical reforms, although initially essential for reducing southern political and economic power, had become an obstacle to northern industrialists and bankers and their grand schemes for ruling the nation as a whole. Black voters and politicians were seen as potential opposition to business policies on issues of internal improvements, tariffs, public services, labor relations, and land allocation. Forty acres and a mule was not what the industrialists and bankers that now dominated the GOP had in mind for the agricultural Black Belt of the South.

These business interests were ready to make an

agreement with the former Confederates to cut Radical Reconstruction short. The power brokers were prepared to abandon the Republican Party's alliance with blacks and take on the planter aristocracy as junior partners in the exploitation of the South, even if this meant restorating the political power of white supremacy. And why not? Most of the northern industrialists and financiers were white supremacists themselves.

Blacks did not by themselves—and they were increasingly by themselves—have the numbers, the economic power, or the political leverage to avert the inevitable. They would soon suffer the fate one can imagine of a racial minority in a nation steeped in racism. As the "strange fruit"[9] began to hang more frequently from southern trees, the nation chose to see no evil, hear no evil, or speak no evil.

Time was running out on the incredible decade that stretched from the Emancipation Proclamation to the reelection of President Ulysses S. Grant in 1872. America's most far-reaching attempt at democratization and empowerment would fail—not because blacks floundered in elective office, or because they were corrupt, or because they had been duped by white carpetbaggers and scalawags. No, Reconstruction fell because America was not prepared to complete the unfinished business of the democratization it so proudly hailed to the rest of world. Even worse, it deserted those black citizens who were prepared.

BETRAYAL AND DEFEAT

Democracy Rejected/White Supremacy Redeemed

It was the chilly early morning of February 27, 1877. The representatives of Rutherford B. Hayes, governor of Ohio and Republican candidate for president, sat down, pen and paper in hand, and began drafting their understanding of the agreement that had been reached late the night before. It had been the wrap-up session of three grueling days of meetings with the leaders of southern Democrats in the House and Senate.

This would be a deal cut in a smoke-filled backroom to top all deals cut in smoke-filled backrooms involving the "Good Old Boys" network. The lesson was evident obvious: some people will do anything to get elected. Rutherford B. Hayes had just done anything.

Southern Democrats were willing to shift their support to Hayes if in return he folded the federal government's hand in the high-stakes poker match between democracy and white supremacy in the Deep South. "Hmmm," Mr. Hayes must have wondered. "Be president, or be principled?" His answer was clear: he'd rather be president, which meant he would withdraw federal troops from the South and his administration from the principle of federal enforcement.

Stalemate in the 1876 Presidential Election

The 1876 campaign had pitted Republican Rutherford B. Hayes against New York lawyer Samuel J. Tilden, the Democratic standardbearer. It was a bitterly fought contest in which support for the Republican ticket had been eroded both by the graft and scandals associated with the outgoing Grant Administration and the slow economic recovery from the Panic (depression) of 1873. Republicans also had not recovered from the defection of liberal Republicans in the 1872 election, including prominent radicals like Charles Sumner. In addition, voices within the party demanding that the Republicans abandon Reconstruction had grown stronger.

Hayes started his campaign pledging to continue Grant's Reconstruction policy, which was not much of a concession since Grant's Reconstruction program had been weak and inconsistent. As election day neared, Hayes all but dropped any pretense of a commitment to "defend and protect the Constitution" in the Deep South. Tilden for his part flailed against the "tyranny of Black Reconstruction" and the "excesses" of the federal government.[1]

When the tally was taken, Tilden had 4,300,590 popular votes, Hayes 4,036,298. Tilden also led in the Electoral College 203 to 169, and so claimed victory. The Republicans disputed the results. In particular, they challenged the outcome in South Carolina, Florida, Louisiana, and Oregon. Without these states, Tilden's electoral vote count dropped to 184 while Hayes's rose to 185, enough to win the presidency in the Electoral College.[2]

The dispute over the results lasted nearly four months. Unless a breakthrough was forthcoming by March 4, 1877, inauguration day, the country would be without a duly elected president. The impasse was broken on that fateful day in February when Hayes, acting through emissaries, promised southern Democrats that he would remove federal troops, provide ample appropriations for internal improvements, and open the public domain in the South to speculators and large scale landholding.[3]

With this pledge in hand, southern congressional Democrats threw their support to Rutherford B. Hayes. No matter that it was contrary to the national interests of the Democratic Party, or that it displayed open contempt for the interests of the rest of the party. Thus did Ohio's undistinguished governor become the undistinguished nineteenth president of the United States. He even failed to inform black Republicans, Frederick Douglass included, of either his intention or his deed.

The Federal Government Abandons the Ex-slaves

The Hayes-Tilden Compromise was the cruelest in a long line of historic compromises with southern racism. It was the compromise to top a century of compromises. This time the treachery was directed against the very concept of "government of the people, by the people, and for the people"—*all* the people.

A Republican president had stabbed in the back his party's most loyal constituency that for two and a half centuries had thirsted for liberty. In less than one hundred words, the betrayal of Reconstruction was signed, sealed, and delivered; it would set back African-American progress for one hundred years. In another irony, this conspiracy was hatched just as the nation had begun preparations for a glorious centennial celebration of the Declaration of Independence. By the Fourth of July, 1876, the Hayes administration had withdrawn federal troops. Counterrevolution was in full swing. Soon each of the states of the old Confederacy would declare themselves "redeemed."

Betrayal and Defeat

The counterrevolution ousted the ex-slaves and their white allies from state houses and state legislatures, city halls and the halls of Congress, county commissions and county courthouses throughout the South. White allies of the freed slaves who came South from the North were called

86

"carpetbaggers"; those native to the South bore the label "scalawags." African Americans in the North lost ground as well. In the space of a few months, the Reconstruction governments were overthrown and democracy lay prostrate before an alliance of southern Democrats and northern Republican backsliders. The black ink on the "gentlemen's agreement" caused the red blood of countless African Americans to run freely and frequently. A week after the compromise of 1877 was reached, Rutherford B. Hayes became president of the United States. Less than a month after that, President Hayes began withdrawing the federal troops that the Reconstruction Act of 1866 had deployed in the states of the former Confederacy. A month later the Supreme Court, in gutting the Fourteenth and Fifteenth amendments, formally and severely restricted the federal enforcement powers that Hayes had relinquished voluntarily.

Within days of the first withdrawal of the federal troops, which had been stationed in Charleston, South Carolina, an armed contingent of white supremacists led by former Confederate officers stormed the state legislature and commandeered the governor's mansion. Daniel Chamberlain, the deposed governor, denounced Hayes's compromise "as a proclamation to the country and the world that the will of the majority of the voters of a state, lawfully and regularly expressed, is no longer the ruling power in our states, and that the constitutional guaranty to every state in this Union of a republican form of government and of protection against violence, is henceforth ineffectual and worthless."[4]

With the federal government looking the other way, Congress no longer interested in Reconstruction, and the Supreme Court once again possessed with racist venom, force and violence were used to carry out various "plans"— each modeled after the Mississippi Plan. Terrorism prevented blacks from voting, and armed insurrections drove the Republican Party underground and eventually out of the region. "Every Democrat," M.W. Gary, a former

Confederate general, proclaimed, "must feel honor bound to control the vote of at least one Negro, by intimidation, purchase, keeping him away or as each individual may determine, how he may best accomplish it. . . . Never threaten a man individually. If he deserves to be threatened, the necessities of the time require that he should die."[5]

Collapse of the Reconstruction Coalition

What produced the betrayal? Simply put, the political alliance that had supported the war of liberation and initiated Reconstruction disintegrated on the rocks of its own internal conflicts. The industrialist capitalists, who were an essential component of the antislavery and Reconstruction coalition, had deserted the cause once they concluded that Radical Reconstruction was too radical. Then, as westward expansion resumed, small farmers, settlers, fortune hunters, speculators, and robber barons questioned using federal troops to ensure African American rights in the South when they could be used to forcibly displace Native Americans from their lands. Last, social reformers no longer saw the Republican Party as an appropriate vehicle for political action, and the more the Republican party became a big business party, the more Republican policy alienated workers and farmers of the North and West. This also cost Reconstruction an essential pillar of mass support. As an increasing number of working-class and middle-class voters outside the South left the Republican Party for the Democratic Party, they realigned themselves objectively with the southern Democrats, who had been steadily regaining strength since the 1867 and 1869 by-elections.

The Republican Party tried to compensate for its losses by further currying favor with white southerners. With the numbers of white Republicans dwindling rapidly, national Republican leaders jettisoned the party's image as the party of the blacks. Southern blacks found themselves increasingly alone. Without the firm hand of the federal government, and faced with a Republican Party in full retreat, they lacked the institutional political power, economic resources, police protection, and military forces to turn back the racist onslaught. Benjamin Wade, at the time one of the few remaining Radical Republicans in Congress, said with remorse:

> I feel that to have emancipated these people and that to leave them unprotected would be a crime as infamous as to have reduced them to slavery when they were free. And for Hayes to do this to the men who had at the hazard of their lives given him the votes without which he could never have had the power to do this terrible injustice: No doubt he meditates the destruction of the party that elected him.[6]

The Redeemed South

The defeat of Reconstruction dealt a devastating blow to the prospects of African Americans. Over the next two decades, a rigid structure of racial separation was imposed on them. White supremacy reigned supreme in theology, sociology, and history. Once again African Americans had no rights a white man was bound to respect.

By the turn of the century, blacks had been purged almost totally from the voter rolls. The constitutions of southern states were altered in open and flagrant violation of the Fifteenth Amendment. In Mississippi, South Carolina, and Louisiana, those who could not pay a poll tax could not vote; neither could those whose grandfathers had not voted before 1868 (the grandfather clause), nor those who had been convicted of a felony, nor "persons who could not read or give a reasonable interpretation of any section of the state constitution."[7]

Many southern states also instituted some version of the notorious "white primary," which permitted only white Democrats to vote in the Democratic primary. Since most of the South was a one-party region, the winner of the primary was assured of winning the general election. Blacks were denied not just the right to vote, but also the right to participate in the political process.

South Carolina adopted the white primary in 1896; Georgia followed in 1898; Florida and Tennessee in 1901; Alabama and Mississippi in 1902; Kentucky and Texas in 1903; Louisiana in 1906, Oklahoma in 1907; Virginia in 1913; and North Carolina in 1915. The impact of the white primary was evident in Louisiana, where 130,334 African Americans voted in the 1896 election; less than a decade later, only 1,342 voted—a 97 percent drop in voter participation.[8] At the turn of the century, Alabama's adult African-American population numbered about 350,000 people; yet only 3,500 blacks were permitted to vote. In Georgia, only about 10,000 out of 370,000 blacks voted; in Virginia, only 15,000 out of over 250,000; and in Mississippi, fewer than 1,000 of more than 300,000.[9]

Plessy v. Ferguson: "Separate But Equal"
The rubble of Reconstruction filled every channel through which the African American tributary once flowed. The denial of democracy to African Americans diminished the level of democracy for all as the great fortunes of unscrupulous industrialists and bankers came to dominate American life during the last quarter of the nineteenth century. "Robber barons" had their way on every issue. Labor organizing stalled. The populist movement succumbed to racism and receded to the fringes of politics. The women's movement became diverted into an isolated channel, at odds with ertswhile allies. Genocide drained Native Americans of their capacity to resist.

A 1896 Supreme Court ruling, which cited the *Plessy v. Ferguson* case, brought down the final curtain on this drama. Enunciating its infamous "separate but equal" doctrine, the court ruled that government-enforced segregation in public accommodations was a "reasonable use of the regulatory powers of the states," adding that "The object of the Fourteenth Amendment was undoubtedly to enforce the absolute equality of the two races before the law, but in the nature of things it could not have been intended to abolish distinctions based on color, or to enforce social, as distinguished from political equality, or a commingling of the two races upon terms unsatisfactory to either."[10]

Only one justice dissented from this decision. In a bitter opinion, Justice John Marshall Harlan, a long time friend of Frederick Douglass, denounced the majority:

> It is, therefore, to be regretted that this high tribunal, the final expositor of the fundamental law of the land, has reached the conclusion that it is competent for a State to regulate the enjoyment by citizens of their civil rights solely upon the basis of race. In my opinion, *the judgement this day rendered will, in time, prove to be quite as pernicious as the decision made by this tribunal in the Dred Scott case [author's emphasis].*[11]

THE GREAT DEBATE OVER GOALS AND DIRECTION

Booker T. Washington vs. W.E.B. DuBois

End of an Era

On the afternoon of February 20, 1895, Frederick Douglass attended a meeting of the National Council of Women. A tumultuous standing ovation greeted him as he entered the meeting hall. That evening, while sitting in a favorite parlor chair engaged in pleasant after-dinner conversation with his wife, Helen, in their home in Washington, D.C., Douglass slumped forward and collapsed to the floor, suffering a fatal heart attack.

He had lived his last day as he had lived his life—in vigorous association with one of the great progressive causes of his times. It was the end of an epoch. The African-American community's great torchlight of clarity and resolve was no more.

Douglass was laid to rest with hero's honors. Grief swept African-American communities across the nation. They mourned for this great American who had held aloft the banner of emancipation, equality, and enfranchisement through a half-century of trials and triumphs.

A year before his death Douglass penned a stinging indictment of the Republican Party's betrayal of Reconstruction and the federal government's complicity in the restoration of white supremacist rule in the South. Entitled *Lesson of the Hour*, it could well be called his last testament. With customary wisdom, Douglass wrote:

> Strange things have happened of late and are still happening. . . . When the moral sense of a nation begins to decline, and the wheels of progress to roll backward, there is no telling how low the one will fall or where the other will stop. The downward tendency, already manifest, has swept away some of the most important safeguards of justice and liberty. The Supreme Court, has, in a measure surrendered. State sovereignty is essentially restored. The Civil Rights Bill is impaired. The Republican party is converted into a party of money, rather than a party of humanity and justice. We may well ask, what next?[1]

The Atlanta Compromise

What was next would become clear six months later. Booker T. Washington, president of the Tuskegee Institute in Alabama, which he had established in the 1880s to provide industrial education for African Americans, made the most celebrated speech of the decade—celebrated, that is, by those seeking to revoke gains made by black labor. To the plantation owners, textile barons, export merchants, financiers, and conservative politicians assembled at the Atlanta Exposition of Cotton States, Washington declared: "agitation of questions of social equality is the extremist folly." Above all, he dismissed Reconstruction, saying:

> Ignorant and inexperienced, it is not strange that in the first years of our new life we began at the top instead of at the bottom; that a seat

in Congress or the State legislature was more
sought than real estate or industrial skill; that
the political convention or stump speaking had
more attractions than starting a dairy farm or
truck garden.[2]

The speech came as another Mississippi Plan—this
one utilizing a literary test and an "understanding" clause
to disfranchise black voters—was being imitated throughout the South. Yet here before the assembled dignitaries of
the southern white power structure, Booker T. Washington
was encouraging the very forces that had excluded black
Americans from the political process and, using sharecropping, tenancy, contract labor, and prison gangs, had
forced them into the new slavery of serflike peonage.

Looking at the throng of gentlemen and ladies with
tearful eye, Washington issued his now infamous invitation
to the rich and powerful to exploit black labor:

> To those of the white race who look to the
> incoming of those of foreign birth and strange
> tongue and habits for the prosperity of the South,
> were I permitted, I would repeat what I say to
> my own race, "Cast down your bucket where you
> are." Cast it down among the 8,000,000 Negroes
> whose habits you know, whose loyalty and love
> you have tested. . . . Cast it down among those
> people who have, without strikes and labor wars,
> tilled your fields, cleared you forests, built your
> railroads and cities, and brought forth treasures
> from the bowels of the earth and helped make
> possible this magnificent representation of the
> progress of the South.[3]

After a century of militant progressive black leadership, at last here was a black man the landed aristocracy could appreciate. Doubtless, they were ecstatic upon
hearing Booker T. Washington say:

As we have proved our loyalty to you in the past, in nursing your children, watching by the sick-bed of your mothers and fathers, and often following them with tear-dimmed eyes to their graves, so in the future, in our humble way, we shall stand by you with a devotion that no foreigner can approach, ready to lay down our lives, if need be, in defense of yours; interlacing our industrial, commercial, civil, and religious life with yours in a way that shall make the interests of both races one. In all things that are purely social we can be as separate as the fingers yet as one hand in all things essential to mutual progress.[4]

The segregationists immediately recognized that Booker T. Washington's "Atlanta Compromise" fit in the tradition of the Missouri Compromise, the Compromise of 1850, and most of all, the Hayes-Tilden Compromise of 1877. White supremacy was uniting southern whites and overwhelming the class politics and incipient interracial solidarity of the populist movement. It even forged a congressional bipartisan unity on racial matters. "There was but one thing needed," Robert H. Brisbane noted. "Some black man with a voice capable of reaching the Negro masses must be found; he must tell them to abandon their futile fight and to attempt to improve themselves in strict accordance with the social and economic rule prescribed for them by the white South. . . . This man was Booker T. Washington."[5]

The Tuskegee Machine
Largely because of the support given his "Tuskegee Machine" by prominent white political and business figures, Booker T. Washington's leadership was virtually unchallenged for the next fifteen years. He was the "race leader" who so thoroughly dominated life in the black community that rarely did an African American receive

even a petty appointment without his approval. The African-American community was restructured according to his strategy of accommodation to the racist status quo. He prescribed industrial training for the African-American masses, opposed higher education for blacks, and favored developing a business or managerial elite ("black captains of industry," he liked to call them) under his tutelage.

Washington especially rejected political action and not infrequently ridiculed African Americans—even to the extent of beginning his speeches to white audiences with a few "darky" jokes. In most instances he was also silent when terrible outrages were committed against the black community. He said nothing about the *Plessy* v. *Ferguson* decision, the Mississippi Plan, or for the most part, the growing number of lynchings and race riots.

The Tuskegee Machine capitulated to racism and was a brake on the development of independent organizations and militant movements. It preached obedience to the powers that be, when defiance and political mobilization were essential.

Opposition to Accommodation Emerges

Opposition to Washington emerged slowly. It was centered at first among a small group of black intellectuals. Organized into the American Negro Academy (ANA), these individuals considered themselves ideological descendants of Frederick Douglass. Although most ANA members were based in the North, they had counterparts in the South. The ANA insisted that Reconstruction was not a failure and demanded full political, economic, and social equality for black Americans.

Among the American Negro Academy's leading voices were Bishop Alexander Crummell, its first president; W.S. Scarborough, a classical scholar who took particular offense at Washington's rejection of higher education for blacks; and W.E.B. DuBois, Harvard University's first African-American Ph.D., whose dissertation, *The Sup-*

THE GREAT DEBATE OVER GOALS AND DIRECTION

pression of the African Slave Trade, was a pioneering work on the consequences of slavery. John L. Love, another leading figure, authored the first scholarly refutation of white supremacist versions of Reconstruction.

The most notable black intellectual in the South to challenge the Tuskegee Machine was John Hope, a professor of classics at Atlanta University. He later became the president of Atlanta Baptist College, which was eventually renamed Morehouse College and two generations later would graduate Martin Luther King, Jr. Hope insisted that "The Negro must enter the fields of higher learning. He must be prepared for advanced and original investigation. The progress, dignity, and respectability of our people depend on this."[6]

The earliest, most direct challenge to Washington came from Monroe Trotter, son of a black Civil War veteran who, though born in Ohio, lived in Boston after graduating from Harvard. Trotter waged an unrelenting, intense political and rhetorical war on Booker T. Washington. In 1901 he and a colleague, George Forbes, founded the *Guardian* newspaper to put "equal rights above party or personal selfishness." They headquartered it in the same building that had housed William Lloyd Garrison's *Liberator;* their message was unmistakable: a new generation of abolitionists had arrived.

W.E.B. DuBois sought to develop an intellectual and programmatic alternative to Washington. He countered Washington's concept of a single race leader with the notion of group leaders, the "Talented Tenth," consisting of highly educated and committed black men and women who would undertake to educate and organize African-American masses. In 1903 DuBois published a collection of essays, *The Souls of Black Folk*. In one essay, entitled "Of Mr. Washington and Others," DuBois delivered a balanced but nonetheless blistering critique of Washington's doctrine and its consequences. "Honest and earnest criticism from those whose interests are most nearly touched," he wrote, "criticism of writers by readers, of government by those governed, of leaders by those led—this is the soul of democracy and the safeguard of modern society."[7]

DuBois termed Washington's thesis on self-improvement a "dangerous half-truth" that ignored the debilitating legacy of slavery and the ongoing role of racial prejudice. He said that Washington's doctrine encouraged whites, North and South, to blame the victim for the consequences of slavery and segregation "when in fact the burden belongs to the nation." For this reason, DuBois said, blacks were duty-bound to oppose "a part of the work" of their "greatest" leader.

> So far as Mr. Washington preaches Thrift, Patience, and Industrial Training for the masses, we must hold up his hands and strive with him. . . . But so far as Mr. Washington apologizes for injustice, North or South, does not rightly value the privilege and duty of voting, belittles the emasculating effects of caste distinctions, and opposes the higher training and ambition of our brighter minds,—so far as he, the South, or the Nation does this,—we must unceasingly and firmly oppose them.[8]

The Souls of Black Folk had an electrifying impact on African Americans. The intimidating veil surrounding Booker T. Washington seemed to be lifted. The book suggested to many blacks that they could live with dignity. Still, the most difficult task remained: the rebuilding of the democratic movement for racial justice. For this, a theory of struggle and a program of action had to be developed in keeping with the new conditions of the twentieth century.

Again W.E.B. DuBois took the initiative. From July 11 to 13, 1905, he assembled on the Canadian side of Niagara Falls leading African-American activists to launch a "permanent national forward movement." Led by DuBois and Monroe Trotter, the purpose of the Niagara Movement was to bring about "organized, determined, aggressive action." The new organization articulated a vision of an inclusive democracy and sought to inspire a higher level of struggle for equality and social justice.

> We want the laws enforced against rich as well as poor; against capitalists as well as laborers; against white as well as black. . . . We want the Constitution of the country enforced. We want Congress to take charge of the Congressional elections. We want the Fourteenth Amendment carried out to the letter and every state disfranchised in Congress which attempts to disfranchise its rightful voters. We want the Fifteenth Amendment enforced and no state allowed to base its franchise simply on color. . . . These are some of the chief things we want. How shall we get them? By voting where we may vote; by persistent, unceasing agitation; by hammering at the truth; by sacrifice and work.[9]

As an organization, the Niagara Movement was short-lived, but as a political thrust and ideological initiative, it was enduring. The Niagara Movement was the immediate forerunner of the National Association for the Advancement of Colored People, which was founded in 1909 by W.E.B DuBois and a host of the country's leading democratic reformers and social activists, black and white.

The Niagara Movement reopened the channels of the African-American tributary; the movement was able to flow again. W.E.B. DuBois navigated much of this travail. From publication of *The Souls of Black Folk*, his years as editor of the NAACP's *Crisis*, the publication of *Dusk of Dawn*, his work with The World and Africa and the Peace Information Center until his death on the eve of the 1963 March on Washington, "W.E.B." provided intellectual guidance, organizational impetus, and mentoring for several generations of African-American freedom fighters.

SOWING THE SEEDS OF A BOUNTIFUL HARVEST

Regroupment and Renewal of the African American Movement

As the twentieth century opened, the overwhelming majority of African Americans lived in rural areas of the Deep South, especially in the fertile crescent running from western Georgia through Alabama and Mississippi to the northern and eastern portions of Louisiana. For the most part blacks living in this Black Belt were sharecroppers and dirt farmers; most were very poor.

The mechanization of agriculture, which had just begun to hit the South, would have a profound impact on the demographics of black Americans. In the new century's first two decades, hundreds of thousands of blacks were dislodged from the land as neither sharecropping nor tenant or subsistence farming could compete with the more efficient agricultural technology. Dispossessed rural blacks headed to the cities, first of the South and then the North, where they found segregated, congested housing, inadequate social services, unscrupulous landlords, and predatory merchants, but also urban culture, an all-encompassing religious life, public education, and a militant political discourse.

The entry of the United States into World War I also helped to transform African-American life. For one thing, the war increased already acute labor shortages, leaving manufacturers and armament producers with no recourse but to recruit blacks to work in their mills, mines, and factories. With manufacturing jobs opening up in the North, where blacks could live in conditions remarkably different from the rigid segregation of the South, and with access to cars, buses, and trains, many blacks "caught the first thing smoking" and headed North. The exodus of large numbers of African Americans out of the South had begun.

The Great Black Migration of the 1920s

Between 1900 and 1920, more than one million blacks moved to the North and West.[1] The rural-to-urban pattern also occurred in the South. By the mid-1920s, a majority of African Americans living in the South were city dwellers. The number of African Americans employed in basic industry during this period nearly doubled, from 500,000 to over 900,000. The number of black steelworkers alone grew from 37,406 to more than 100,000.[2]

Blacks were hired at the lowest rungs of the job ladder and worked in the worst conditions, at the lowest wages. The racial discrimination they experienced, which was closely linked to class exploitation, differed profoundly from the South's racial caste system in which blacks and whites were segregated in everything from employment to toilets, from drinking fountains to cemeteries. In the South a black sharecropper might work year-round from "can see to can't see," only to end up owing a plantation owner, absentee landlord, or company store more than he or she had earned in the entire year. The resulting indebtedness kept them bound to their employers. In the North, although as a rule making less than whites, blacks pulled

the weekly wages of steel, auto, rubber, electrical, or pack-
inghouse workers. They lived in squalid tenement housing or neighborhoods milked dry by white slumlords. They
also encountered the enmity of police, who thought of
themselves as overseers, if not overlords.[3] Even so, blacks
had a freedom of movement and employment in the North
that was unknown in the South.

The arrival in the cities of so many blacks in such a
short period of time created huge social problems, rang-
ing from housing shortages to inadequate public services.
Migration, urbanization, and industrialization forced black
institutions and civil rights organizations to broaden their
focus from traditional concerns with legal and political
rights to issues of discrimination in hiring, wages, and
working conditions. They also had to persuade organized
labor to adopt a firm stance against racial discrimination.

By the mid-1910s the NAACP was making aggressive attempts to cooperate with labor unions. The National
Urban League was established in 1912 to help newly arriv-
ing blacks adjust to northern urban settings; it also worked
closely with employers to recruit southern blacks for northern industry.

Not all black organizations were pro-union. Booker
T. Washington and Robert R. Moton, his successor as president of Tuskegee Institute, were vehemently antiunion.
They advised blacks to break strikes and to refuse to join
unions. Marcus Garvey, a onetime disciple of Washington,
and his Universal Negro Improvement Association, a black
nationalist back-to-Africa movement that at one point had
several million members, held white workers and unions
in open contempt. Garvey argued that black workers, sure
to be sold out by white trade unionists, should make common cause with white employers by working for lower
wages than whites.

Black Workers and Organized Labor
The racial exclusion practiced by most unions at the time
did not help endear them to the black community. Most

labor organizations were white-led and nearly all-white or entirely white. Many unions with black members had racially segregated locals. The large-scale entry of African Americans into mass-production industries challenged the longstanding practices of organized labor *and* the entrenched prejudices of white workers.

Employers could get away with job discrimination, residential segregation, and union-busting as long as the American Federation of Labor took a passive approach to their racist practices and did not rid itself of racial bias. Ten years after the first Great Black Migration had peaked, and in spite of the presence of more than one million African Americans in the mass-production industries, blacks still had been unable to gain entry into most of America's labor unions.

Although racial prejudice was widespread within the AFL, racism was not the sole reason for this. It is true that many AFL leaders opposed organizing industries with a large number of African-American workers and that the AFL catered to the racial prejudices of white workers to retain their support. But the AFL also organized workers by craft, not industry. This meant AFL unions were concerned primarily with skilled workers, and skilled workers were overwhelmingly white. African Americans were concentrated in industries where unions were far and few between. A democratic, not an elitist, labor movement would have to be built. Otherwise the work force, black as well as white, would be unprotected.

The New African American

Migration to the North and to big cities and finding work in mass-production industries raised black aspirations. Their expectations of first-class citizenship accelerated the growth of protest sentiment. This new consciousness was expressed in a growing body of distinctly urban music, art, and literature. The period between the two world wars witnessed a series of African-American cultural movements—the Harlem Renaissance, the Black Renaissance,

103

the International Negritude Movement, and the New Negro. Jean Toomer, Richard Wright, Langston Hughes, Claude McKay, Margaret Walker, James Weldon Johnson, and Zora Neale Hurston were among the distinguished cultural figures to chronicle black life and protest in poems, novels, stories, and plays.

As the 1930s gave way to the 1940s, jazz and other forms of popular black music became more explicitly political. This was especially true of "be-bop," a jazz idiom developed by Charlie Parker and Dizzy Gillespie. Blues songstress Billie Holiday sang the antilynching ballad "Strange Fruit." Paul Robeson's famous baritone reverberated with the "Ballad of the Americans" and Negro spirituals. Duke Ellington wrote many of his jazz suites to inspire racial solidarity. These and scores of other brilliant African-American men and women pioneered the consolidation of an authentic African-American national culture, which was integral to the broader American culture.

On the scholarly front, W.E.B. DuBois's *Dusk of Dawn* and his monumental study, *Black Reconstruction*, documented African-Americans' achievement. He edited the journal *The Crisis* from the NAACP's founding until 1934, and then again for a short time in the late 1940s., to rally the American people against racial abuse.

Great Depression and Great Discrimination

The nation's financial system collapsed when the stock market crashed in October 1929, throwing the United States into its longest and deepest economic crisis. The Great Depression was just that, great and depressing. By 1932 unemployment had swelled to more than 15 million, wages had dropped 45 percent, and those living below the poverty line rose from 40 percent to 75 percent of the population.

At the depth of the depression, 25 percent of the civilian labor force was out of work. Although millions were homeless and starvation stalked the land, little in the way of help came from the federal government. Most city and county governments provided only the bare minimum in public assistance. Unemployment compensation did not exist. Neither did welfare, food stamps, Social Security, old-age pensions, Medicare, Medicaid, a forty-hour work-week, minimum wage, or collective bargaining rights.

If things were bad for whites, they were much worse for blacks. In some cities, black unemployment hovered around 50 percent. By 1932 40 to 50 percent of Harlem's blacks were unemployed, 56 percent of Philadelphia's, 40 percent of Chicago's and Detroit's, and 50 percent of Gary, Indiana's. In 1933 34 percent of blacks in Chicago and Philadelphia were on relief; 43 percent in Cleveland; 67 percent in Akron, Ohio; and 60 percent in St. Louis.[4]

Many African Americans had been the last hired in many industries; now they were the first fired. Before the Depression there were "Negro jobs"—the ones so dirty, so hard, and so low in pay that most whites would not take them. When the hard times hit, whites considered them "our jobs." Even black domestic workers lost their jobs to whites or as a result of the plummeting incomes of the well-to-do. Employers also used joblessness to reduce wages; blacks saw theirs drop by about one-third.[5]

The collapse of agricultural prices, especially for cotton, bankrupted and ruined tens of thousands of black farmers and sharecroppers. This prompted another 300,000 African Americans to migrate north during the depression years. Hard times awaited them in the cities. Rampant discrimination in the administration of relief payments left millions of African Americans on the brink of starvation. Kelly Miller, a Howard University sociologist, wrote that "fully a third of the race is unemployed and another third under-employed," while the Urban League reported that blacks were "hanging on by the barest thread."[6]

From Reluctant to Enthusiastic Supporters of Roosevelt

The Republicans held the White House when the Depression hit. President Herbert Hoover did very little to alleviate the destitution gripping the country. He was adamantly opposed to federal welfare programs, believing that the federal government had no business providing work or relief to the unemployed or the poor. He lost his reelection bid by a landslide to Democrat Franklin Delano Roosevelt, but still pulled two-thirds of the black vote. Although Roosevelt swept forty-two of the then forty-eight states, taking 472 electoral votes to Hoover's 59, he had not done as well among black voters as Al Smith, the 1928 Democratic nominee.[7]

Two factors explain why blacks stayed with Republicans. First, Roosevelt barely distinguished himself from Hoover in his proposals to deal with the Depression; he did not run on a platform of radical change, and only proposed a "New Deal" in his inaugural speech (he did not begin undertaking it until nearly the end of his first term). Second, like most northern Democrats of his day, Roosevelt courted the South. At the 1932 convention, he rejected the NAACP's request for a plank on civil rights.

Of course, Roosevelt did face a predicament; southern Democrats dominated the leadership of House and Senate committees, and the fate of his anti-Depression legislation would depend on their support. Their price was hands-off the South's "way of life."

African Americans found little to praise and much to complain about during most of the first Roosevelt administration. The President's initial New Deal—especially the National Recovery Administration (NRA) and the Agricultural Adjustment Administration (AAA)—were turned into instruments of exploitation and oppression.[8] No steps were taken by the Administration to restrain landlords and employers from cheating or discriminating against African Americans. As Harvard Sitkoff writes,

> . . . In the North racist employers, trade unions, and city officials flagrantly disregarded non-discriminatory rules promulgated in Washington. Worse yet for blacks, the day-to-day

106

management of the New Deal in the South, where three-quarters of the Negroes still lived, remained in the hand of the hierarchy that had traditionally oppressed Afro-Americans and still stood to profit by discriminating against blacks.[9]

The Great Depression and the Struggle for Racial Equality

Despite these shortcomings, something profound and powerful was brewing underneath these limited New Deal programs. Grassroots movements fighting for radical reforms began to sprout up. Tens of thousands of activists came forward to provide militant leadership to workers in factories, on farms, and in the community. African Americans were not lacking in initiative; they took an active role in the Unemployed Councils, union organizing drives, and in farm tenant movements.

These popular movements demonstrated their strength in the 1934 midterm congressional elections. The results transformed the political composition of Congress and provided Roosevelt with a mandate and the votes for a genuine "new deal." In 1935 the new Congress passed the National Labor Relations Act (Wagner Act), granting private sector workers the right to organize unions, bargain collectively, and strike. This produced a surge in new union organizing, largely by the newly-established Congress of Industrial Organizations, which was led by John L. Lewis of the United Miner Workers, a union well-known for organizing black workers on a nondiscriminatory basis.

Congress also passed the Social Security Act, which created unemployment compensation and a retirement benefits system. In 1938 it adopted the Fair Labor Standards Act, which established the forty-hour work week and a minimum wage and outlawed child labor.

Roosevelt's New Deal was now in full swing; between 1934 and 1939 the Works Progress Administration (WPA), Civilian Conservation Corps (CCC), and National Youth

Administration (NYA) were put into place, each of which provided public service and public works jobs for millions of the unemployed. Roosevelt also created the Tennessee Valley Authority, the Rural Electrification Administration, the Federal Land Bank, and the Farm Security Administration, programs that brought electricity, paved roads, stable prices, and relief to vast rural areas of the South.

Black Voters Change Parties

Although African Americans continued to encounter discrimination in these and other New Deal programs, they were clearly among their major beneficiaries as well. This consolidated the historic shift in black voting behavior that began with the 1934 midterm election. It had been the first in history in which a majority of blacks voted Democratic.

Several factors figured in breaking the loyalty of blacks to the party of Abraham Lincoln. The Roosevelt administration had begun to find its voice on issues of racial equality—primarily due to First Lady Eleanor Roosevelt's singular role in urging her husband, his administration, and the country to face up to the persistence of racism. Blacks were also pleased with the direction of the Roosevelt administration, and blacks sensed their potential importance to the New Deal coalition, and the Democratic Party, more than the Republican Party, realized that the African-American electorate could contribute the margin of victory in critical elections.

Black candidates also scored impressive breakthroughs in the 1934 election; they won important local offices in Detroit, Cleveland, New York, and in Chicago, where Arthur Mitchell defeated Oscar DePriest to become the first African-American Democratic member of Congress. Mitchell's slogan was a sign of the changing times: "Forward with Roosevelt."[10]

African Americans were indeed moving forward; under Roosevelt the number of blacks in the federal labor force grew from about 50,000 in 1933 to nearly 200,000 in 1946. More than 200,000 young African-American men and women were involved in the Civilian Conservation Corps. Another 64,000 black youth, 10 percent of the total, were enrolled in the National Youth Administration's student work-study program. In 1939 alone, more than one million blacks were in employed in the WPA.[11]

Roosevelt also had a "black Cabinet"—an informal network of African-American advisers. Mary McLeod Bethune, a close personal friend of Eleanor Roosevelt, may have been the most influential black in the Roosevelt Administration. Other key African-American advisers included Eugene Kinckle Jones of the National Urban League; William H. Hastie, dean of Howard University's Law School;, and Robert C. Weaver, an expert on housing, who years later in the Kennedy administration became the first African-American Cabinet member.[12]

The CIO and the Struggle for Racial Equality

The Congress of Industrial Organizations was the first national labor organization in American history to back up its stated policy on racial equality with tangible deeds. The CIO focused on organizing workers in basic industry, precisely where African Americans were heavily concentrated. In this way it brought large numbers of African-American workers into the labor movement.

Many of the leaders and organizers of the CIO were Communists, socialists, or radicals of various stripes, activists whose commitment to racial equality was very much like that of the abolitionists a century earlier.[13] In addition, CIO organizers knew that mass-production industries could not be organized if African-American workers were excluded. In many situations black votes made the difference between victory and defeat for the union.[14]

The CIO's organizing drives in steel, auto, rubber, electrical, meatpacking, and other basic industries—the strength of the country's economy—enjoyed such phenomenal success that the AFL was forced to take up the challenge of industrial unionism in order to keep pace with its rival. Between 1932 and 1939, the total membership of unions surged from three million to almost nine million. By 1940 the AFL had about six million members and the CIO over four million.[15]

The growth in African-American union membership between 1935 and 1945 was nothing short of spectacular. Before the CIO was founded, scarcely 100,000 African Americans belonged to unions; by World War II nearly 500,000 did.[16] By the end of the war, more than one million African Americans were members of unions, mainly those affiliated with the CIO.

Sowing the Seeds of a Bountiful Harvest

The African-American community found a new and powerful ally in the CIO. John Hope Franklin writes that,

> . . . the CIO's organizing campaigns in many industries brought higher incomes, better working conditions, and some measure of job security for hundreds of thousands of black workers —with the participation of black workers themselves—than it had in almost a century of previous existence.[17]

The CIO's organizing successes, and particularly its political muscle, intensified the momentum of the New Deal and gave impetus to further civil rights progress. The unprecedented degree of multiracial unity the CIO brought to the workplace, voting booth, and legislatures also solidified pro-union sentiment in the African-American community.[18]

While blacks were active in the labor movement, black activism was on the rise in a myriad of organizations; for instance, the National Negro Congress, NAACP, Urban League, American Youth Congress, and Southern Negro Youth Congress (the first "Snick"). Left-wing organizations, particularly the Communist Party, which distinguished itself in the fight for racial equality and in building multiracial unity, gained a substantial following among blacks. Demands increased for enactment of a federal anti-lynching law, as well as prohibition of the poll tax, and other procedures to disfranchise African Americans.

African Americans staged massive protest actions against the Italian invasion of Ethiopia. They fought and died in the Abraham Lincoln International Brigade, which fought on the side of the antifascist forces in Spain. They stood up against the frame-up of the Scottsboro Nine—a group of black Alabama teenagers sentenced to be executed for fabricated rape charges. They defended Angelo Herndon, a black Unemployed Council organizer in Georgia, who defiantly told his accusers, "You can kill me, but you can't kill the working class."

African Americans and the FDR Coalition

The future of the New Deal depended not only on mass movements, but also on keeping Roosevelt in the White House and a progressive majority in the House and Senate. Blacks overwhelmingly supported Roosevelt's 1936 reelection campaign. He took 76 percent of the black vote overall and won at least 60 percent in every big northern city, except Chicago where he still gained more than 50 percent.

Roosevelt's coattails were wide and long as New Deal Democrats trounced their conservative opponents, Democrat and Republican alike. Non-southern Democrats were now a clear majority among the Democrats in both the House and Senate. The South accounted for thirty of sixty Senate Democrats in the Seventy-third Congress (1933–34) and thirty of sixty-nine in the Seventy-fourth Congress (1935–36), but only thirty of seventy-six in Seventy-fifth Congress (1937–38). Southerners comprised 130 of 311 Democratic representatives in the Seventy-third Congress and 130 of 320 in the Seventy-fourth Congress, but just 130 of 331 in the Seventy-fifth Congress. The presence of thirteen third-party members in the House and four in the Senate in the Seventy-fifth Congress (1937–38) only increased the South's isolation.

It was a situation analogous to the Fortieth Congress

111

that launched Radical Reconstruction. President Roosevelt could pass his New Deal legislation without the help of southern Democrats. Moreover, southern conservative Democrats could not count on the support of every southern Democrat, for a new force had emerged in southern politics: southern liberals. Though relatively small in number, southern liberals occupied positions of influence in the press, academia, the arts, and elective office. The combination of southern liberals and the resurgence of the African-American protest movement meant that the battle for economic reform and civil rights progress would be carried into the South increasingly by southerners.

With President Roosevelt's approval and Eleanor Roosevelt's personal involvement, the Southern Conference for Human Welfare (SCHW) was held in November 1938 in Birmingham, Alabama. At the same time, the Southern Negro Youth Congress was preparing a generation of black youth to demand full equality. The SNYC may have been the single most effective organization in bringing progressive politics to southern African-American youth. In the civil rights upsurge of the 1950s and 1960s, hundreds of former SNYC members led the way.

Cross Pollination of Movements and Concepts

The New Deal, industrial unionism, a resurgent civil rights movement, and left-wing radicalism contributed to the onrushing currents of the African-American tributary in a number of ways. First, African-American participation in the labor movement brought militant, skilled organizers to the African-American community. Second, the CIO's organizing drives gave the most visionary of African-American leaders a keen appreciation of the power of mass direct action.

Third, the CIO's prestige among white workers enabled it to build mass white support in unions and the larger society for its stance on racial equality. Fourth, by inaugurating an era of democratic reforms and broad coalitions, the New Deal consolidated an alliance between organized labor, the African-American community, and liberal Democrats to achieve greater civil rights progress.

Fifth, labor law reform enacted under the New Deal undermined states' rights on the one hand, but strengthened federal regulatory policies and redistributional programs on the other hand. African-American leadership quickly grasped the relevance of those New Deal agencies and programs for the struggle for racial equality.[19] If the federal government could regulate labor-management relations and intervene in the economy to promote social justice, it could do the same for racial justice. In fact, the National Labor Relations Board, set up in 1935 under the National Labor Relations Act, would serve as the model for the Equal Employment Opportunity Commission. This was the administrative agency that civil rights advocates eventually won under the Civil Rights Act of 1964.[20]

For its part, the Roosevelt administration took limited steps in this direction. In 1939 U.S. Attorney General Frank Murphy created the Civil Rights Division of the Justice Department to "direct, supervise and conduct prosecutions of violations of the provisions of the Constitution or Act of Congress guaranteeing civil rights to individuals."[21] In 1941 President Roosevelt, under pressure from A. Phillip Randolph's threat of a massive march on Washington, issued the pioneering Executive Order 8802, creating the Fair Employment Practices Commission (FEPC).[22]

Although the FEPC lacked administrative resources and did not have statutory powers or clearly defined jurisdictional authority, federal regulatory powers had been applied for the first time to the enforcement of an antidiscrimination statute.[23] It was also the first executive order since the Emancipation Proclamation to be issued in connection with eliminating racial discrimination. Whatever its inadequacies, the FEPC spurred the civil rights movement to seek companion state legislation, most of which did establish enforcement agencies with mandated statutory powers.

CIVIL RIGHTS UPSURGE

"And Justice Will Roll Down Like Waters From A Mighty Storm"

Black veterans—many of them members of the Southern Negro Youth Congress—returned home from World War II demanding freedom for which blacks had fought and died overseas.[1] Local protest organizations quickly sprouted up throughout the North and particularly the South. African Americans were inspired by the successes of the independence movements that were sweeping Africa, Asia, and the Middle East. Witnessing the ambassadors of the new nations taking their seats in the newly formed United Nations, black Americans were even less willing to accept second-class citizenship.

In 1949, with the Cold War confrontation between the United States and the Soviet Union reaching a fever pitch, members of the Civil Rights Congress, spearheaded by Paul Robeson and William L. Patterson, carried petitions with hundreds of thousands of signatures to the United Nations charging the U.S. government with committing genocide against African Americans and other racial minorities in the United States.

For their own reasons, of course, the more far-sighted U.S. corporate leaders and foreign policy specialists understood that segregation handicapped the United States' ability to present itself as a bastion of democracy and freedom. They knew that "Old Jim Crow had to go," but they just could not get white southerners to agree.

Blacks were ready for a major assault on racial discrimination and white supremacy, but the Cold War and McCarthyism delayed the new phase of African-American mass action. Radical black thinkers and activists were a special target of McCarthyite politicians. Accused of being a Communist, Paul Robeson was brought before the House Un-American Activities Committee; his passport was seized for eight years; and his access to stage and screen dried up, depriving him of the ability to earn a livelihood in his profession.

In 1951 at age eighty-two, W.E.B. DuBois, the venerable scholar and intellectual patriarch of the African American community, was indicted, arrested, handcuffed, and locked up on charges of being a "foreign agent."[2] Only an international outcry and the outrage of the black community prevented the government from pressing its trumped-up charges.

Many mainstream black organizations joined the anticommunist chorus.[3] The NAACP, for instance, did not lift a finger to aid Dr. DuBois, one of its principal founders; such was the intimidation that McCarthyism imposed on the country, the African-American freedom movement included. McCarthyism had the effect of a gag order on many of the most farsighted leaders of the black community.

Nonetheless, the buildup of protest continued. The NAACP won a series of key cases during the 1940s: the Supreme Court held that the white primary was unconstitutional (*Smith* v. *Allwright*, 1944) and found that the unequal funding of racially separate school systems violated the equal protection clause of the Fourteenth Amendment (*Sipuel* v. *Oklahoma, 1948)*.[4]

The Brown Decision: A Crack in the Levee of Oppression

Largely as a result of these successes and aggressive action at the grassroots level, the NAACP's ranks swelled to 500,000 members by war's end.[5] During the 1940s, the NAACP Legal Department, first headed by Charles Houston and then Thurgood Marshall, fashioned a strategy of challenging the entire system of Jim Crow segregation. This meant overturning *Plessy* v. *Ferguson* and its "separate but equal" doctrine.

Roosevelt died in the spring of 1945 and was succeeded by Harry Truman, his vice president and a conservative Democrat. The commitment of the Democrats in Congress to the New Deal began to fade. In the 1946 midterm election, the Republicans gained control of the House and Senate, and promptly united with southern Democrats. From now on, as far as this conservative coalition was concerned, the business of Congress was going to be big business. The growing power of the labor movement was checked when, over Truman's veto, Congress passed the Taft-Hartley Act in 1947, which severely restricted the ability of unions to conduct new organizing drives. This was a preemptive blow against Operation Dixie, the coordinated organizing drive planned jointly by the AFL and the CIO.

Southern Democrats once again wielded extraordinary power in the congressional committee system. Matters could not have looked worse. In 1952 Dwight D. Eisenhower, a former general and war hero turned Republican candidate, won the presidency. "Ike" did not look favorably on civil rights. He sought instead to build the Republican Party in the South by appealing to the segregationist vote. To further complicate matters, the Supreme Court repeatedly delayed taking up "separate but equal" cases. All three federal branches seemed allied against civil rights progress.

Then in early September 1953, Chief Justice Fred Vinson—the court's chief civil rights obstructionist—died of a heart attack. Eisenhower, in what he later called the "worst damn fool mistake" he had ever made, appointed California governor Earl Warren, a Republican, to replace Vinson as Chief Justice.[6]

Six months later, on May 17, 1954, in *Brown* v. *Board of Education of Topeka, Kansas*, the Supreme Court ruled unanimously that racially segregated schools were inherently unequal, and therefore, unconstitutional. Earl Warren not only wrote the opinion, but also mobilized the consensus.[7] Thurgood Marshall's strategy had been victorious. In terms of impact, this historic decision overturned the legal underpinnings of the entire Jim Crow system.

The *Brown* decision raised the expectations of African Americans dramatically. With *de jure* discrimination (discrimination by law) outlawed, they set their sights on ending *de facto* discrimination (discrimination by practice). Over the next decade and a half, they would secure unprecedented legal, legislative, and political victories that would be called the Second Reconstruction.[8]

A year after the *Brown* decision, the Supreme Court ordered school systems to desegregate with "all deliberate speed." The South rapidly went from all deliberate delay to Massive Resistance to desegregation. In 1957 circumstances compelled a reluctant Eisenhower to send federal troops into Little Rock, Arkansas, to force authorities to comply with court-ordered desegregation.

Flood Stage: The Dam Breaks in Montgomery
The events in Little Rock showed that Brown had been only the first significant crack in the levee of oppression; the damn of segregation had yet to be broken. That would happen in Montgomery, Alabama, "the Cradle of the Confederacy." December 1, 1956, was an apparently normal workday. Late that afternoon a middle-aged African-American seamstress named Rosa Parks, a respected, church-going member of the community and former youth secretary of the Alabama NAACP, was taking a bus home after a long, hard day on the job. When the "whites only"

seats were filled, the bus driver ordered Parks and the other blacks on board to give up their seats and go to the back of the bus. The others went. Rosa Parks didn't. She just said, "No." She said later that her feet were "too tired." The bus driver had her pulled from the bus and arrested.

Word of Parks's arrest spread like wildfire. The black community was virtually unanimous; the segregationists had gone too far, and Montgomery's black citizens had had enough. On December 5, African Americans under the leadership of the Montgomery Improvement Association, began a boycott of the entire bus system. For the next 381 days it held 95 percent solid as blacks walked to and from work, car-pooled, or took taxis. The boycott cost blacks collectively a quarter of a million dollars in transportation fares, a small price to pay for dignity and justice.

The segregationists retaliated against the leaders and supporters of the boycott. Soon after the Reverend Martin Luther King, Jr., a young minister, was chosen to head the Montgomery Improvement Association. Soon his home was firebombed. At one time or another, all the leaders of the boycott were jailed and countless boycott members were fired from their jobs. The Alabama state legislature banned the NAACP for having filed a federal lawsuit against the Montgomery bus service. The Montgomery Improvement Association was fined $100,000 for operating the car-pool without a license. The hardships were severe, but the boycott continued as an elderly black woman said, "My feets is tired, but my soul is rested."

Then, on November 13, 1956, the Supreme Court upheld a lower court decision that declared that Alabama's state and local laws requiring segregation on buses were unconstitutional. A month later, the Montgomery city authorities agreed to desegregate the city bus service. On the morning of December 21, 1956, Martin Luther King, Jr., and his colleagues in the Montgomery Improvement Association boarded a bus, and sat in the front, side by side with whites. A sweet victory had been won.[9]

The Meaning of Montgomery

Dr. Martin Luther King, Jr., emerged from the Montgomery boycott as a national civil rights leader. He was a "reluctant warrior" who had assumed the presidency of the Montgomery Improvement Association at the prodding of E.D. Nixon, a veteran of a generation of struggle for racial justice in the Black Belt and a leader of the Brotherhood of Sleeping Car Porters. King's leadership signaled the adoption of a multifaceted protest strategy derived from the techniques and philosophy used by Mahatma Gandhi to gain India's independence from Great Britain.[10] It featured total mobilization of the black community and its resources, and the formation of multiracial coalitions. Nonviolent resistance and direct action were employed to develop "creative tension" that would "compel unwilling authorities to heed the mandate of justice," and culminate in negotiation and reconciliation.

The progressive political activism of black clergy, which dated back to the time of the black abolitionists and Reconstruction, was revived with the Montgomery boycott. Critics have scoffed at the religious overtones of this movement and its strategic and philosophical commitment to nonviolence. But what other choice did African Americans have? Any other course would have been counterproductive. Even in the Black Belt counties where African Americans were a numerical majority, hostile white authority had a monopoly of power and force. King pointed out that this approach "was the only morally and practically sound method open to oppressed people in their struggle for freedom."[11]

A just cause can, King said, "meet physical force with soul force." King was able to make the principles and program of the African-American struggle unassailable from the standpoint of the Declaration of Independence and the United States Constitution. " . . . the great glory of American democracy," he said during the Montgomery boycott, "is the right to protest for right."

> There will be no crosses burned at any bus stops in Montgomery. There will be no white persons pulled out of their homes and taken out on some distant road and murdered. There will be nobody among us who will stand up and defy the Constitution of this nation.[12]

The Montgomery boycott was all the more daring and democratic because it occurred in the midst of McCarthyism. King fended off charges that the movement was "communist-inspired." "If we are wrong," he observed with typical eloquence, "the Supreme Court of this nation is wrong. If we are wrong the Constitution is wrong. If we are wrong the Declaration of Independence is wrong. If we are wrong—God Almighty is wrong."[13]

The Struggle Continued

From the mid-1950s to the late 1960s, the civil rights revolution swept through the South and headed North. African Americans, other racial minorities, and growing numbers of white allies challenged the political arrangements that underpinned racial discrimination. One Jim Crow edifice after another was swept away by the onrushing democratic currents. Each success deepened the struggle and broadened its vision.

In 1957, the same year President Eisenhower sent federal troops into Little Rock to quell segregationist resistance, Congress passed a modest civil rights bill that created the U.S. Commission on Civil Rights, which could recommend legislation to the president and the Congress; this legislation also formally established the Civil Rights Division of the Justice Department and authorized the Justice Department to bring suit on behalf of citizens denied the right to vote. Congress adopted another civil rights measure in 1960, which made obstruction of a federal court order by violent means a federal crime; it also gave federal courts the power to appoint referees to safeguard voting rights.[14]

The Founding of the SCLC and SNCC

The momentum of the Montgomery boycott led directly to the founding of the Southern Christian Leadership Conference in January 1957. Its purpose was to provide coordination and leadership for a new generation of educated activist clergy that had taken command of the civil rights movement in the Deep South. Some say that the energy and initiative that Martin Luther King and the SCLC brought to the African-American freedom movement surpassed that of even the venerated NAACP.[15]

A youth movement within the civil rights movement was sorely needed. Black youth would soon find their unique way of contributing to the struggle. On February 1, 1960, four first-year black students at North Carolina A & T University—Joseph McNeil, Izell Blair, Franklin McCain, and David Richmond—sat in at the lunch counter of a Woolworth's store in Greensboro, North Carolina. Thus began the sit-ins that challenged segregation in public accommodations throughout the South. By that April an estimated 50,000 students, mostly black but also a good number who were white, had taken part in sit-ins, boycotts, wade-ins, pray-ins, and picketing of segregated facilities around the nation.[16] Like the Montgomery boycott, the student sit-in movement had a profound effect on the consciousness of the black community. It helped as well to transform the outlook of the white youths of the 1960s, turning many of them toward political activism.

The sit-ins were the stimulus for the creation of a new youth organization, the Student Non-Violent Coordinating Committee (SNCC). "Snick" (as the organization was called) was founded at a civil rights conference, April 16–18, 1960, at Shaw University in Raleigh, North Carolina. The idea for an independent youth organization came from Ella Baker, then executive director of SCLC, who realized that the students needed to learn how to sustain their movement. She also hoped to inspire the students to be organizers "who are interested not in being leaders as much as in developing leadership among other people."[17]

SNCC pioneered the transition from the desegregation struggle to that for voting rights. In Howard Zinn's words, SNCC activists were the "new abolitionists" who dared to undertake tasks that would lead to beatings, prison, and sometimes even death. The brutal murder in June 1964 of James Chaney, a local black Mississippi SNCC worker, and Andrew Goodwin and Michael Schwerner, two Jewish New Yorkers who were volunteers in the Mississippi Freedom Summer voter registration project, came to symbolize the self-sacrifice and courage of SNCC.

Freedom Rides

In early 1961, the Congress of Racial Equality (CORE) revived the Journey of Reconciliation, which it originally had attempted in 1948 to desegregate bus terminals in the North. Now called the Freedom Ride, its purpose was to test compliance with *Boynton* v. *Virginia*, the Supreme Court decision that racial segregation was illegal in all interstate commerce—not only on trains, buses, and planes, but also in terminals, rest rooms, and waiting areas.

On May 4, 1961, thirteen specially recruited black and white volunteers, some from CORE and the others from SNCC, left Washington, D.C., in two groups, one aboard a Greyhound bus and the other on a Trailways, bound for the Deep South. John Lewis, a future member of the House of Representatives, was among them. Theirs was a supremely dangerous mission. Massive resistance had whipped white southerners into a racist frenzy precisely in the states the Freedom Riders had to cross to get to New Orleans: Virginia, North Carolina, South Carolina, Georgia, Alabama, Mississippi, and Louisiana. Woe be unto those daring to break the line of racial demarcation that had segregated public schools, textbooks, libraries, public transportation, toilets, water fountains, and even graveyards for seventy-five years!

The Freedom Riders were beaten in South Carolina, and again in Anniston, Alabama, where one of their buses was burned by an unruly mob outside of town. They were arrested in Birmingham, released, and sent on to Montgomery, where some of them were again beaten severely. Some of the original Freedom Riders were too battered to continue. SNCC activists took their place. In Jackson, Mississippi, when the Freedom Riders tried to access the "white" waiting room, they were beaten, arrested, beaten again, and thrown into the dreaded Parchment Prison, where those who adhered to a "jail/no bail" code served three-month sentences for "disturbing the peace."

None of the original thirteen Freedom Riders made it to New Orleans, but the Freedom Ride did. Prominent Americans from all over the country joined; others undertook solidarity Freedom Rides. That September, the Interstate Commerce Commission ruled that interstate carriers could not use the terminals that violated its ban on segregation. They had to comply or face heavy fines and go out of business. Another levee of racial proscription had been washed away.

Impact of Civil Rights on the 1960 Elections

By the time the 1960 presidential election rolled around, television had brought the drama of the Montgomery bus boycott, the Little Rock desegregation crisis, the sit-in movement, insurrectionist governors, and racist mobs into the homes of tens of millions of Americans. These scenes enabled the American people to see for themselves what was going on and draw their own conclusions about segregation and the social order. Public opinion demanded stronger civil rights legislation and federal protection for civil rights protesters. Civil rights had become the crucial subtext of the 1960 presidential contest between moderate Democrat John F. Kennedy and conservative Republican Richard M. Nixon, Eisenhower's vice-president.

Throughout the campaign the NAACP, SCLC, CORE, SNCC, and the Urban League pursued a common strate-

123

gy of pressuring the candidates to respond to the movement's insistence on stronger civil rights statutes. These
organizations hoped to emerge from the election with an
alliance of the civil rights movement and the federal government, and, specifically, a president more favorably dis-
posed toward civil rights than Eisenhower.

The hopes of civil rights leaders soared when Kennedy
was elected. During the campaign he had sympathized
publicly with the civil rights movement, even calling King's
wife, Coretta, to offer assistance while Dr. King was in
jail in Albany, Georgia. Kennedy won by the closest margin
ever. Black voters had given him overwhelming support.
However, as president, Kennedy was a disappointment to
the civil rights community and especially to SNCC, which
was enduring some of the severest blows from the racist
power structure in the rural South.

To a certain extent Kennedy was hamstrung by the
political balance in the Congress. The 1960 election had
cut Democratic strength in the House and Senate, leaving him dependent on the cooperation of southern congressional Democrats. He was legitimately afraid that an
aggressive civil rights policy would alienate them and hurt
his reelection chances in 1964; but he was also a calculating politician who thought he could get away with not
taking risks on this question.

Life forced Kennedy's hand. On September 10, 1962,
Supreme Court Justice Hugo Black ruled that James
Meredith must be admitted to the all-white campus of the
University of Mississippi in Oxford. Governor Ross
Barnett, citing the doctrine of interposition and nullifica-
tion, which asserted that states were sovereign and there-
fore had the right to cancel federal action if they pleased,
personally barred Meredith's admission.

This insurrectionary act precipitated the worse fed-
eral-state crisis since the Civil War. Kennedy had no choice.
He sent federal marshals to the University of Mississippi
to force its compliance with Justice Black's order. A mob of
thousands of white students and Oxford townspeople, led

by former general Edwin Walker, attacked the federal marshals. Two people were killed and more than one hundred were wounded. Kennedy responded by sending 12,000 federal troops to restore order. Meredith was enrolled. Walker was arrested on charges of inciting insurrection.[18]

Breakthrough in Birmingham

"The Battle of Oxford" made President Kennedy even more reluctant to take the offensive on civil rights. Martin Luther King and SCLC concluded that the Kennedy administration's backsliding would never break the South's resistance to desegregation. In April 1963, King launched a coordinated campaign to desegregate the city of Birmingham, Alabama, long a symbol of segregation. SNCC also intensified its voter registration efforts in rural Mississippi. These two campaigns constituted a program for the democracy that African Americans had sought for so long. By coincidence, the year was the 100th anniversary of the Emancipation Proclamation.

King believed that the President should no longer be allowed to express concern for civil rights while doing little, when new policies, legislative programs, and strict enforcement were clearly needed. King also hoped to create a chain reaction that would shatter the Jim Crow system throughout the South.

The objective in Birmingham was "to create a situation so crisis-packed that it will inevitably open the door to negotiation" between the city's power structure and the movement. A segment of Birmingham's black establishment refused to support King's campaign, fearing the results would ruin their somewhat privileged relationship with the establishment. The black working class, however, gave its enthusiastic support. Where some adults were hesitant, black youth and schoolchildren marched eagerly. They faced police dogs, high-pressure water hoses, and Police Chief Bull Connor's billy clubs, eventually embarrassing or inspiring the older generation to join in.

King was arrested on Good Friday for defying an

injunction against one of the marches. A few days later, the *Birmingham News* headlined a story: "White Clergymen Urge Local Negroes to Withdraw from Demonstrations." In reply, King addressed to them the now famous "Letter from a Birmingham Jail."[19] To those who called the Birmingham Movement "untimely," King replied:

> Frankly, I have yet to engage in a direct-action campaign that was "well-timed" in the view of those who have not suffered unduly from the disease of segregation. For years now I have heard the word, "Wait!" It rings in the ear of every Negro with piercing familiarity. That "Wait" has almost always meant "Never." We must come to see, with our distinguished jurists, that "justice too long delayed is justice denied."[20]

Bull Conner's brutality had shocked the nation and the world. A national consensus on civil rights progress was taking shape. Public opinion demanded that the federal government intervene, and Kennedy had to act. While he wanted to hold his own in the South in the coming election, he also knew that his reelection would more likely depend on how he responded to the demand of millions of Americans of all colors for federal action against racist violence.

Kennedy felt international pressure as well. The Soviet Union had broadcast 1,420 commentaries worldwide on the crisis in Birmingham, and the summit conference of the Organization of African Unity, in response to his message of greetings, had protested the "snarling dogs" of Birmingham.[21] In addition, he faced the prospect of a massive civil rights march on Washington, which had been called for late August 1963.

Kennedy's emissaries urged the city's business establishment—particularly the U.S. Steel Corporation in Birmingham—to make genuine concessions. Birmingham's business circles concluded that segregation was not as profitable as it had been. CEOs of major corporations with offices or investments in the South saw the business value in ending segregation.

By the end of May, Birmingham authorities had agreed to desegregate all public facilities, and business leaders agreed to hire and promote African-American workers on a nondiscriminatory basis. A biracial committee was set up to monitor implementation of the agreements and to work out additional steps.

Black militancy surged from Birmingham into nearly every black community in the country. By autumn of that year, nearly 15,000 people had been arrested for taking part in almost 1,000 marches, sit-ins, and boycotts in about 200 cities and towns across the South. In many places, formal agreements to desegregate public accommodations were reached.[22]

King's "Letter" had been prophetic. "Abused and scorned though we may be," he had written, "our destiny is tied up with America's destiny. . . . If the inexpressible cruelties of slavery could not stop us, the opposition we now face will surely fail." Public opinion polls all during the summer showed that an overwhelming majority favored laws that guaranteed the voting rights of African Americans; that penalized discrimination in employment; that would assure equal opportunity; and that actually desegregated schools and public accommodations.[23]

The Civil Rights Act

In June, Kennedy announced that he would submit to Congress the most far-reaching civil rights bill in the country's history. Kennedy underscored his new stance by dealing forcefully with Alabama when its governor, George Wallace, tried to obstruct a federal court order to integrate the University of Alabama.

The evening of the day the first two black students in history had enrolled at the University of Alabama, a member of a white supremacist group shot and killed Medgar Evers, state field secretary of the Mississippi

NAACP, in front of his home in Jackson. This happened only hours after John F. Kennedy had become the first president since Abraham Lincoln to address the nation on the issue of racism.

"It is a moral issue," the President told the country, "as old as the Scriptures and as clear as the Constitution." He emphasized that 100 years after the Emancipation Proclamation black Americans "are not yet freed from social and economic oppression. . . . It is a time to act, in the Congress, in your state and local legislative body, and, above all, in all our daily lives."[24]

The March on Washington

Originally, a march on Washington was to mobilize support for civil rights, creation of jobs, and equal employment opportunity. As events turned out, it would center on building support for President Kennedy's proposed civil rights legislation. Although the march itself went smoothly, the road to Washington was bumpy.

SNCC wanted to demonstrate at the Justice Department to protest the Kennedy administration's ineffectiveness in protecting civil rights workers, and CORE agreed. SCLC proposed a massive sit-in that would bring the nation's capital to a standstill. The NAACP and Urban League would have none of this, and after learning that Kennedy opposed the march, Roy Wilkins, the NAACP's longtime executive director, demanded a rally, without civil disobedience, full consultations with the Kennedy administration, and the removal of Bayard Rustin as march chair on grounds that he was "too radical" or, Wilkins inferred, gay, which ironically could jeopardize congressional support for civil rights.[25] Wilkins had the others over a barrel. They could not go ahead without the NAACP because it would fracture the unity of the black community. The NAACP's absence also would have reduced the potential impact of the march on Congress.

Other controversies swirled around the March on Washington. The Kennedy administration feared things would get out of hand and wanted it canceled. The AFL-CIO refused to have anything to do with it. Afterward, Malcolm X, who had done nothing to build the march, called it the "farce on Washington."

The great masses of African-American people, however, had another opinion. Every conceivable type of organization or institution in the black community contributed to the mobilization. Despite the AFL-CIO's position, the American Negro Labor Council pressured unions with a large number of African-American members to become involved. Unions like the United Auto Workers, the American Federation of State, County and Municipal Employees, and, of course, the Brotherhood of Sleeping Car Porters mobilized.

On the day of the march, August 28, 1963, everything had come together. Almost all the streams of black protest and interracial solidarity that fed into the African-American tributary flowed into the nation's capital that day. More than 250,000 Americans, an estimated 20 percent of them white, converged in front of the Lincoln Memorial and along the sides of the Reflecting Pool. They came by train, plane, bus, and car, and some walked. For every person who attended, there were probably a hundred who wanted to go. Churches, foundations, unions, civic groups, fraternities and sororities gave generously. Nickels and dimes had been collected in barbershops, beauty parlors, bars, and social clubs.

As the program began, it was announced that just hours earlier W.E.B. DuBois had passed away in Ghana, where he had gone to live out his years advising the revolutionary government of Kwame Nkrumah as well as working to complete the *Encyclopedia Africana*. In 1957 DuBois penned a message that was to be opened after his death. It said in part,

> . . . always I have been uplifted by the thought that what I have done well will live long and justify my life; that what I have done ill or

never finished can now be handed on to others for endless days to be finished, perhaps better than I could have done.

And that peace will be my applause.

One thing alone I charge you. As you live, believe in life! Always human beings will live and progress to greater, broader and fuller life.

The only possible death is to lose belief in this truth simply because the great end comes slowly, because time is long.[26]

Symbolically, the death of W.E.B. DuBois on the eve of the March on Washington signaled the passing of the torch of leadership to a new generation. This legacy, which stretched from the *Amistad* mutiny, through Denmark Vesey and Nat Turner, to Harriet Tubman and Frederick Douglass, to DuBois and Paul Robeson, was present in the dignity of the assembled masses.

Yet, as the program wore on, the spirit of DuBois seemed to bypass the platform and speakers. John Lewis, the chairman of SNCC, who two decades later would be elected to the House of Representatives, excited the crowd even though he did not give the speech he had prepared. Lewis had wanted to express the "great sense of misgiving" of the radicalized black youth of SNCC who, at their peril, were toiling in the political vineyards of the Black Belt. The initial draft was a strident critique of the Kennedy administration that rejected the President's civil rights bill as "too little, too late." He also wanted to proclaim that "the revolution is at hand," and therefore, the need to "create a source of power, outside of any national structure."[27] By rejecting an alliance with the Kennedy administration, Lewis's speech broke with the civil rights coalition's consensus on strategy and goals.

Several other passages so enraged key march supporters that some threatened to walk off the platform if Lewis gave the speech as written.[28] After much negotiation, Lewis agreed to make changes. The modified version stated SNCC's case forcefully. In retrospect, this episode was indicative of divisions that were yet to come.

The last speech of the day was that of the Reverend Dr. Martin Luther King, Jr. In it, he constructed carefully a vision of a multiracial democracy. He characterized the Declaration of Independence as a promissory note "to which every American was to fall heir." America had given African Americans a "bad check" which had come back marked "insufficient funds." To thunderous applause, he declared:

> But we refuse to believe that the bank of justice is bankrupt. We refuse to believe that there are insufficient funds in the great vaults of opportunity of this nation. So we've come to cash this check—a check that will give us upon demand the riches of freedom and the security of justice.

King presented a blistering critique of gradualism and the politics of the status quo, insisting instead on a militant approach to the next phase of the struggle. "We have also come to this hallowed spot," he said, "to remind America of the fierce urgency of now. This is no time to engage in the luxury of cooling off or to take the tranquilizing drug of gradualism. *Now* is the time to make real the promises of democracy."[29]

King then spoke of having a dream that was "deeply rooted in the American dream"—a society in which its citizens "will not be judged by the color of their skin but by the content of their character." In the tradition of DuBois and Douglass, King gave leadership not just to African Americans but to the nation as a whole. In the space of about eight minutes, he had given hope and direction to a troubled nation. He had spoken within the existing civil rights consensus while at the same times extending its vision of an inclusive, multiracial democracy.

The March on Washington consolidated a new national consensus without which passage of the Civil Rights Act of 1964 and the Voting Rights Act of 1965 might not have been possible. The march, together with King's "I Have A Dream" speech, shifted the initiative from the moderates within the civil rights movement to Martin Luther King, Jr., and the SCLC. King and SCLC presented more far-reaching challenges to the political and economic status quo in which discrimination was embedded.

Although SNCC would help to spearhead the new wave of challenges, the March on Washington also revealed that SNCC leadership did not understand the nature or the extraordinary potential of the national consensus that August 28, 1963, had achieved. Nor did Malcolm X, the most vocal critic of the march, and Malcolm X exercised considerable influence on SNCC's orientation.

To the left of Martin Luther King, neither Malcolm for all his brilliance, nor SNCC for all its incipient radicalism understood that as long as the unity of the main forces involved in the mobilization for the March on Washington was strengthened, the consensus could be deepened, the coalition against racism and discrimination broadened, and the struggle for equality intensified. To King and SCLC's right, neither the NAACP nor other civil rights establishment forces appreciated the need to deliver ever more decisive blows against poverty and institutional racism.

Accomplishing these multifaceted tasks required both legislative action and a militant grassroots movements. Unfortunately, even as the mission and methods of the movement were expanding, the outlook of some of its components had narrowed rather than broadened. Looking back more than thirty years later, the 1963 March for Jobs and Freedom stands out as the nation's greatest mass gathering for democracy. In subsequent years, the precedent of the march on Washington would be followed by opponents of the war in Vietnam, the women's movement, organized labor, and others who would measure their protests by its yardstick.

132

FROM CIVIL RIGHTS TO HUMAN RIGHTS

The Movement's Methods and Mission Expand

The assassination of President Kennedy shocked the nation and the world. The prospect of Vice-President Lyndon Baines Johnson, ostensibly a conservative Texan, succeeding him shocked black leaders. "LBJ" had played the key role in watering down civil rights legislation when he was Senate majority leader in the 1950s.[1] As vice-president, Johnson had been kept out of the decision-making on civil rights policy, so few people had a clear idea of where he stood.

Now Johnson was president. The factors that would propel Johnson were both political and personal. He needed to establish his own legitimacy, and unless he stepped out of the shadow of John F. Kennedy's legacy, it was doubtful whether he could be elected in his own right.

The Second Reconstruction

Civil rights was the most compelling issue that confronted the nation and the one on which he would have to stake his presidency. He knew that he could not act like a southerner on civil rights and be regarded as president of all the people.[2] Johnson later recalled "that if I didn't get out in front on this issue they [the liberals] would get me. They'd throw up my background against me. They'd use it to prove I was incapable of bringing unity to the land. . . . I had to produce a civil rights bill even stronger than the one they'd have gotten if Kennedy had lived. Without this, I'd be dead before I could even start."[3]

As it turned out, LBJ, with his New Deal philosophical roots, had a much deeper commitment to civil rights than Kennedy. Now that he was president, Johnson could freely express his view that racism and poverty were the overriding afflictions of the South. He was determined to find policy cures for both. As vice-president, Johnson had built solid personal relationships with civil rights leaders through his work as chairman of the President's Committee on Equal Employment Opportunity. He also had strong ties with labor leaders who were most progressive on civil rights, particularly Walter Reuther, president of the United Auto Workers Union.

These connections served President Johnson well as his administration and the civil rights movement undertook to enact the most far-reaching civil rights and voting rights legislation. What seemed improbable when Johnson took the oath of office hours after Kennedy's assassination began to take shape immediately: the long-sought alliance of the civil rights movement and the federal government. The President made it abundantly clear that he would not tolerate a watered-down bill. He used his knowledge of Congress and his relationships with key Democrats and Republicans to break a fifty-seven-day filibuster (the longest in history) of southern pro-segregationist congressional Democrats.[4]

In mid-June 1964, Johnson's measure, on which civil rights leaders had been fully consulted, passed the Senate by a vote of seventy-three to twenty-seven. The House approved the Senate version on July 2, 1964, by a 289–126 margin. Within hours, President Lyndon Johnson signed the Civil Rights Act of 1964 into law.[5]

Title I of the act made it illegal to apply unequal standards or to administer literacy tests in voter registration procedures. Title II made it unlawful to discriminate against or segregate Americans in public accommodations for reasons of race, color, religion, or national origin.[6]

Title III and Title IV, respectively, authorized the Justice Department to undertake civil action on behalf of persons denied equal access to public accommodations, and persons attempting the orderly desegregation of public schools.

Title V empowered the United States Commission on Civil Rights to investigate voting rights violations and issues studies on discrimination in America.[7]

Title VI prohibited any public or private program, agency, or institution found guilty of discriminatory practice from receiving federal funds. The threat of withdrawing federal funds turned this provision into a powerful compliance mechanism.

Finally, in the most far-reaching antidiscrimination breakthrough in U.S. history, Title VII made it unlawful for any firm or labor union employing or representing twenty-five or more persons to discriminate against any individual in any manner on grounds of race, color, religion, sex, or national origin. It also established a new federal enforcement agency, the Equal Employment Opportunity Commission.[8] The Civil Rights Act of 1964 exceeded all previous civil right legislation in the protections provided to victims of racial and gender discrimination. The provision denying federal funds and contracts to institutions that did not comply with the Act broke the back of southern resistance. It also transformed the federal government from a passive to an active institutional force for racial justice, making the Civil Rights Act of 1964 the enabling legislation of the Second Reconstruction.

Dynamics Surrounding the 1964 Presidential Election

Historically, because black voters were partially or wholly disfranchised, fear of a white backlash and the loss of southern electoral support had inhibited presidential action

135

on civil rights. The Civil Rights Act of 1964 was passed only four months before election day. Lyndon Johnson would discover shortly whether he would be rewarded for doing the right thing.

Danger signs had already appeared: Governor George Wallace of Alabama did surprisingly well in a number of Democratic primaries. Pledging "to make race the basis of politics in this country," Wallace took 34 percent of the vote in Wisconsin, 30 percent in Indiana, and almost 43 percent in Maryland. Now he was threatening to weaken Johnson in the South and Midwest by running as an independent.

Arizona senator Barry Goldwater, an arch-conservative who had voted against the Civil Rights Act, was the Republican nominee. Goldwater opposed practically every policy Johnson favored. By late summer, Goldwater had Wallace's support. Wallace canceled his plans for an independent bid in favor of endorsing Goldwater. A right-wing bipartisan electoral alliance was a distinct possibility. Civil rights leaders knew that a Goldwater victory would abort a Second Reconstruction and reverse the progress that had been made since the *Brown* decision.

To most African-American leaders the choice in this presidential election was clear. This one would not be a case of the lesser of two evils. Nonetheless, the campaign placed African-American leadership in a very difficult situation. The Civil Rights Act had given fresh impetus to the grassroots struggles for racial justice, but blacks could overplay the highly favorable hand that history had finally dealt them if they pushed too hard in such a delicate presidential contest.

The tactical challenge centered around how to make further advances without precipitating a white backlash, and helping Goldwater and hurting Johnson. In a further complication, riots broke out within days of Goldwater's nomination in Harlem and Brooklyn in New York City, then in Philadelphia, Rochester, and Chicago. The Republicans charged the Civil Rights Act encouraged "lawlessness" and that Johnson was "soft on crime."

136

Mississippi Freedom Democratic Party Challenge

While George Wallace was making a strong showing in the spring, black Mississippians were forming the Mississippi Freedom Democratic Party (MFDP) to challenge the seating of the regular state Democratic Party's delegation to the national convention in Atlantic City in August. The segregationist regular party not only excluded blacks from the delegate selection process, but from state politics as a whole.

Johnson feared that if the MFDP was successful, other southern state delegations would walk out of the convention, split the party, and thus cost him the election. He appealed to national civil rights leaders to help avert the MFDP's challenge, citing the obvious fact that he had just helped them win the most advanced ever civil rights bill. The President also wanted a moratorium on demonstrations until after the election in order to avoid handing Goldwater an issue.

Johnson was also worried that SNCC's Mississippi Freedom Summer, a voter registration project that had attracted hundreds of white student volunteers from around the country, would provoke the segregationists to vote against him. He believed that violence against the civil rights workers was inevitable and that he would have to take federal action against white southerners on behalf of blacks on the eve of the election. Three civil rights volunteers, James Chaney, Andrew Goodwin, and Michael Schwerner, did disappear on June 21, the first day of the project. Forty-four days later their bodies were found buried underneath an earthen dam near Meridian, Mississippi, in dreaded Neshoba County.

Civil rights leaders knew full well that black voters in the South could not carry the South for Johnson by themselves; he would need significant white voter support. On their own, the major national civil rights organizations decided to curtail direct action. They also supported a compromise between the Mississippi Freedom Democratic Party and President Johnson—seating the regular delegates if they agreed to support the national ticket, establishing a national party commission to work out nondiscriminatory delegate procedures for future conventions, and giving special status to two MFDP delegates.

These terms were unacceptable to the MFDP. It especially resented the attempt to choose which of its delegates would be seated. To the MFDP delegation, this seemed like the white supremacist arrogance they were fighting in Mississippi. The state-party delegates did not agree to the compromise proposal either. They refused to pledge their support for the national ticket or loyalty to the national party and walked out of the convention.[9]

Although the MFDP delegates did not see it at the time, in retrospect it is clear that they had won a huge moral and political victory that helped set the stage for the unprecedented inclusion of blacks in the Democratic Party over the next decades. The MFDP challenge also added to the momentum that was building in the country and the Congress for new federal voting rights legislation.

The statements of MFDP delegates to the Credentials Committee, particularly the riveting testimony of Fannie Lou Hamer, graphically portrayed the extent of voting rights violations in Mississippi. The political repression state and local authorities imposed on blacks who tried to exercise their constitutional right was revealed to the nation. The MFDP was the first to implement successfully an "inside-outside" strategy—an independent black political mobilization committee inside worked with a third party outside to isolate the regular state party organization nationally.

Black Voters Contribute to Johnson's Victory

Johnson crushed Goldwater. Democratic congressional candidates trounced the Republicans. Goldwater carried his home state of Arizona, plus Alabama, Georgia, Louisiana, Mississippi, and South Carolina; Johnson took the other forty-three. Johnson carried 375 of 435 congressional districts; he had 486 electoral votes compared to Goldwater's 52; and he took the popular vote by a margin of 62 percent to 38 percent. The Republicans lost two Senate seats and thirty-seven House seats, which gave the Democrats a 68 to 32 majority in the Senate and 295 to 140 in the House.[10] Like Ulysses S. Grant and Franklin Delano Roosevelt at their peaks, Johnson would not need the votes of southern congressmen to enact his legislative agenda.

While the results strengthened the national civil rights consensus, they also revealed a partisan realignment and racial polarization of southern politics. Johnson narrowly lost the popular vote in the South, 49 percent to 48.9 percent margin. He did not win a majority of the white vote in a single southern state except his home state of Texas; if not for overwhelming black voter support, LBJ would have lost the whole South. Incidentally, 1964 was the first time since Reconstruction the African-American vote in the South had been large enough to deliver a southern state—Arkansas, Florida, North Carolina, Tennessee, and Virginia.[11]

Blacks in the South supplied almost one million votes for Johnson.[12] This clearly established that they were becoming the mainstay of the Democratic Party in Dixie. Nationwide, 94 percent of the African-American turnout went for Johnson. African Americans played an indispensable role in defeating the leading spokesperson for ultra-right forces.

Even so, the racial polarization of the southern vote marked the beginning of a white backlash that threatened to put the Democrats in the same situation the Republicans had faced during Reconstruction. The Democratic Party might not be able to hold the White House much longer without either enlarging the black vote significantly or doing better among white southerners. Doing both seemed to be impossible as long as blacks insisted on civil rights progress and white southerners resisted.

The role of black voters was not lost on the Johnson administration, or black leadership, especially SCLC and SNCC. More than 700,000 blacks had registered to vote in the South since the sit-ins in 1960. The number of black voters in the region now topped 2.1 million, and over 6 million nationally.[13] These voters had been decisive for Johnson's southern state victories. However, only 41.9 percent of the black voting-age population in the Deep South was actually registered; another three million voting-age blacks were not—primarily because of race-based suppression of their voting rights.

The Struggle for Voting Rights

Coming out of the 1964 elections, black leaders agreed that extending and protecting the right to vote of blacks in the South was the key to the future. The changes that were taking place in the South would be consolidated and a Congress favorable to the adoption of much-needed social programs could be elected. Register the remaining eligible black voters, give them somebody and something to vote for, build multiracial electoral coalitions with white liberals and moderates, and southern as well as national politics could be reconstructed on a genuinely democratic basis. Years before, Martin Luther King, Jr., had already made the case:

> Give us the ballot and . . . we will write the proper laws on the books. Give us the ballot and we will fill the legislature with men of goodwill . . . Give us the ballot and we will transform the salient misdeeds of the bloodthirsty mobs into the calculated good deeds of orderly citizens.[14]

Federal legislation protecting the right to vote was crucial. The partisan interests of the Democratic Party and the democratic interests of African Americans once again were the basis of an alliance for legislative reform. And, once again, the waters of the River of Freedom surged into the mainstream of American politics and widened the democratic rights and constitutional protections of all Americans. New voting rights legislation and its strict enforcement by the federal government would dredge the political process of the debris of disfranchisement that had for so long blocked meaningful African-American participation in public policy making.

The Selma Movement

In January 1965, Martin Luther King launched a series of mass demonstrations in Selma, Alabama, for the right to vote. Having just returned from Oslo, Norway, where he received the 1964 Nobel Peace Prize, he knew that media throughout the world would be closely following his activities. SCLC had spent the months since election day carefully preparing the Selma campaign, which was to be modeled after the Birmingham Movement.

In 1964 only 2.1 percent of the black voting-age population in Selma (353 African Americans) was registered to vote. To register, a person had to go to the county courthouse in Selma, where the board of elections was open only two days a month, and for a short period of time at that. Normally about 75 percent of the handful of blacks who attempted to register failed the board's literacy test.[15]

The Johnson administration monitored the situation in Selma closely. By February, Sheriff Jim Clark had arrested more than 2,000 voting rights protesters, including Martin Luther King, Jr. The *New York Times* published King's "Letter from a Selma Jail," which detailed the scope of the denial of the right to vote in and around Selma. The Reverend James Bevel, a SCLC official, told a rally, "If we get out and work, Jim Clark will be picking cotton with my father in about two years."[16]

Putting aside their differences, SCLC and SNCC had joined forces with the Dallas County Voters League. Supporters were recruited in all the city's wards who canvassed door-to-door for black residents courageous enough to try to register.

As the voter registration movement expanded to rural counties surrounding Selma, differences between SCLC on the one hand, and SNCC and local leaders on the other hand, surfaced. The Dallas County Voters League wanted to change conditions in Selma and Dallas County. SNCC wanted to develop indigenous leadership, and therefore believed the decisions should be made by local leaders. In contrast, the SCLC intended that the Selma Movement should challenge all black disfranchisement and force the Johnson administration to protect the right to vote.[17]

SCLC's rift with SNCC deepened. King had grown increasingly worried that SNCC's desire to confront the local powers would lead it to jettison nonviolence. SCLC's strategy of expanding democracy in America might at one moment require confrontation, at another negotiation, but at all times it adhered strictly to nonviolence and assumed the moral high-ground.

Selma to Montgomery March

The Selma struggle came to a head on March 7—"Bloody Sunday." Six hundred protesters left Brown Chapel in Selma to march to Montgomery, the Alabama state capital, fifty-four miles away. They intended to dramatize the massive disfranchisement of black voters, mobilize public pressure nationwide, and lay the responsibility for voting rights violations squarely on the doorstep of Governor George Wallace. The marchers were also intent on protesting the death of Jimmie Lee Jackson, who had been shot by a state trooper after a voting rights demonstration in nearby Perry County.

After crossing the Edmund Pettis Bridge just outside of Selma, the marchers were set upon by Alabama state troopers and Sheriff Jim Clark's forces. The demonstrators were bombarded with canister after canister of tear gas; club-wielding state troopers and "possemen," some on horseback, charged the march, clubbing men, women, and children to their knees. The leaders of the march, including John Lewis of SNCC, Hosea Williams of SCLC, and Amelia Boynton of the Dallas County Voters League, were beaten severely. Swinging wildly while hundreds of white bystanders cheered their approval, the police chased the marchers back across the bridge all the way to Brown Chapel.

A few days later, several white ministers who had answered King's appeal to join the Selma protest were set upon by racist thugs. One of the ministers, Reverend James Reeb of Boston, died a dew days later.

The Sunday evening TV network news programs showed extensive footage of the brutality. The Monday editions of most newspapers featured Bloody Sunday. National and international reaction was swift in condemning the Alabama state police and Sheriff Clark.

King, who was not present for the march, called on civil rights organizations to flood the White House and Congress with telegrams denouncing the attack. He appealed to supporters to converge on Selma for another march to Montgomery on the following Tuesday.

Across the nation the public demanded federal action and immediate passage of voting rights legislation. Demonstrators marched outside the White House. Clergy descended on Capitol Hill. Solidarity marches and vigils were held throughout the country.

The Johnson administration went into high gear. First of all, the President condemned Alabama State authorities in unambiguous terms for obstructing the right to vote. He assured the country that "the best legal talent in the federal government is engaged in preparing legislation which will secure that right for every American." He dismissed Governor Wallace's claim that King and the demonstrators were the problem. During Wallace's visit to Washington for "consultations," Johnson told the governor that the responsibility of the state of Alabama was to protect, not attack, peaceful protest.

Plans for a second march ran into an unexpected obstacle. Federal Judge Frank Johnson issued an injunction barring the march until he could hold a full hearing on

SCLC's suit requesting a restraining order against the state of Alabama. SCLC, SNCC, and local leaders threatened to march anyway. The Johnson administration interceded with King to change the organizers' minds. At the last minute, King, who was also troubled by the prospect of defying a federal court order—something the civil rights movement had never done—agreed to march across the bridge and, when confronted by state troopers, say a few prayers and return to Brown Chapel.

SNCC and many local leaders were furious, because they had not been consulted. They objected to King's willingness to compromise. SNCC pulled out of Selma and began to stage protest actions in Montgomery. King's decision not to defy the federal court order was a part of the strategy of building an alliance with the federal government against recalcitrant state authorities in the Deep South. Had the protesters marched, the Johnson administration would have been pitted against the Selma Movement, and the enormous pressure on the authorities in Selma and Montgomery would have been removed.

As matters stood, Judge Johnson, one of the heroes of the era, who became renowned for his rulings on constitutional law, found that " . . . right to assemble, demonstrate and march peaceably along the highways and streets in an orderly manner should be commensurate with the enormity of the wrongs that are being protested and petitioned against. In this case, the wrongs are enormous."[18] In abiding by the federal injunction, the Selma Movement had reinforced and expanded the scope of First Amendment protections. In subsequent years other democratic movements would benefit from this ruling.

Two days before Judge Johnson's finding, President Johnson addressed a joint session of Congress on voting rights, which was televised to upwards of seventy million Americans. The President endorsed the Selma protest with these words:

> At times history and fate meet at a single
> time in a single place to shape a turning point

in man's unending search for freedom. So it was at Lexington and Concord. So it was a century ago at Appomattox. So it was last week in Selma, Alabama.[19]

Johnson restated his administration's determination to enact new federal voting rights legislation.[20] But he did not stop here. "What is happening in Selma," he said, "is part of a far larger movement which reaches into every section and State of America. It is the effort American Negroes to secure for themselves the full blessing of American life . . . their cause must be our cause too, because it is not just Negroes but really it is all of us, who must overcome the crippling legacy of bigotry and injustice. And we shall overcome."[21]

"Will wonders never cease?" African Americans all over the country must have asked themselves. One supposes white supremacists pondered the same question from a different point of view. The president, a southerner, in clear, unmistakable terms lauded African Americans as "the real heroes of this struggle" who had "awakened the conscience of this Nation."[22]

On Sunday, March 21, two weeks after Bloody Sunday, by the consent of the federal judiciary, with the backing of the President of the United States and the solidarity of millions of their fellow citizens, 300 marchers led by Martin Luther King, Jr., left Brown Chapel. As they walked without incident through downtown Selma and crossed the Edmund Pettis Bridge, they were joined by hundreds more who had come from all over the country and the world. They were accompanied as well by hundreds of troops from the Alabama National Guard that had been federalized by President Johnson, plus 2,000 U.S. soldiers, 100 FBI agents, and 100 federal marshals.

Scores of people joined them on the way. Hollywood stars entertained them at night. Five days later, the marchers reached Montgomery and walked past the Dexter Avenue Baptist Church, Dr. King's first pastoral assignment and a key organizational depot of the bus boycott.

The hundreds had become thousands. By the time they reached the capitol building, the thousands had become tens of thousands. Their numbers had swelled to 25,000, and some estimate that twice that many filled the plaza. Among their numbers were Rosa Parks of the Montgomery bus boycott, Ralph J. Bunche, the U.N. secretary and the first black to receive the Nobel Peace Prize; the NAACP's Roy Wilkins; the Urban League's Whitney Young; SNCC's John Lewis; A. Phillip Randolph of the Brotherhood of Sleeping Car Porters; Sammy Davis, Jr.; the noted novelist James Baldwin; Rabbi Heschel of the American Hebrew Union; and Walter Reuther of the United Auto Workers.

Every now and then the crowd could see Governor Wallace peek through the venetian blinds of his office window.[23] "We're on the move now," King told the exuberant masses. "Like an idea whose time has come, not even the marching of mighty armies can halt us." He also warned, "We are still in for a season of suffering." He reminded the marchers and their supporters that the justice of their cause and their nonviolent methods had the power to change existing conditions. "I know you are asking today," he continued, "How long will it take?"

> ". . . however difficult the moment, however frustrating the hours, it will not take long, because truth pressed to earth will rise again.
> . . . How Long? Not long. Because the arc of the moral universe is long, but it bends towards justice.[24]

The Second Emancipation Proclamation

How long? Within five months, Congress had passed legislation that was the result of consensus between the Johnson administration and the civil rights movement.

By a 328 to 74 margin it passed the House; the vote was 79 to 18 in the Senate. Congress had finally adopted "appropriate legislation" to implement the Fifteenth Amendment fully ninety-five years after its ratification. On the sixth of August, at an elaborate ceremony in the Rotunda of the Capitol Building, where Abraham Lincoln penned the Emancipation Proclamation, President Lyndon Baines Johnson, in the presence of a broad array of civil rights leaders, members of Congress, and notable personalities, signed the Voting Rights Act of 1965 into law.[25]

The Voting Rights Act mandated an unprecedented degree of federal intervention in the electoral process to guarantee voting rights of racial minorities. It empowered the attorney general to replace local officials with federal registrars and authorized the Justice Department to suspend literacy tests, waive poll taxes, and register voters under simplified federal procedures.[26]

States where literacy tests and other qualifying devices were in use as of November 1, 1964, where fewer than 50 percent of the voting-age population was registered to vote or had cast ballots in the 1964 presidential election were brought under the Act's jurisdiction—Alabama, Arkansas, Georgia, Louisiana, Mississippi, South Carolina, Texas, and Virginia. Later, under the 1975 extension of the Act, counties or cities in Connecticut, California, Colorado, Florida, Hawaii, Idaho, Massachusetts, Michigan, New Hampshire, New Jersey, New York, North Carolina, South Dakota, and Wyoming were added.[27] These states were not permitted to change their electoral procedures without "preclearance" from a special three-judge panel in Washington, D.C., or the Justice Department.

There were but 280 African-American elected officials in the United States in 1965, and only 87 in the South. Only 44 percent of African-American registered voters in the South cast ballots in the 1964 presidential election, compared with 59.6 percent of white registered voters. Only 41.9 percent of the region's black voting age population had been registered to vote.[28]

The impact of the Voting Rights Act was swift and dramatic. In Selma, Alabama, for instance, within two weeks of the Act's passage, 381 blacks had registered to vote—more than the total number who had been registered in the preceding sixty-five years. A year later, more than 9,000 blacks in Selma were registered, enough to defeat Sheriff Jim Clark's reelection bid.[29]

Over the next two years more than 560,000 blacks were registered in Alabama, Louisiana, Mississippi, and South Carolina with the help of federal registrars.[30] By 1970 black registration rates rose to 66.9 percent of the black voting-age population. More than 1.3 million blacks had been added to the registration rolls. There was also a fivefold increase in the number of African-American elected officials, half of whom were in the South—eight times the number that existed when the Voting Rights Act was passed.

By the mid-1990s the country would have nearly 14 million black registered voters and over 8,000 African-American elected officials. Half of these registered voters were in the South. And Mississippi, with 751 African-American elected officeholders, would lead the nation in the number of black elected officials. Meanwhile southerners would account for eighteen of the thirty-nine members of the Congressional Black Caucus.

These breakthroughs in the right to vote and in blacks' increasing ability to elect candidates of their choice did not mean that electoral politics would be the only vehicle the African-American community would use to intensify their struggle for equality. Nor did these breakthroughs resolve all of the problems African Americans faced. There was some progress, however. For example, studies show that the administration of justice, delivery of government services to the African-American community, relations between the police and blacks, and the orientation of public policy tend to improve where African-Americans are voters and hold significant elective offices. The election of African-American officeholders also appears to contribute to the community's greater self-esteem, racial pride, and a sense of being players in the drama of policy making.

African-American political participation also encountered a white backlash. The emerging rejection of further civil rights progress on the part of a growing number of whites was clearly evident in the 1966 midterm congressional election, which saw the Republican Party regain nearly the number of House and Senate seats it had lost in its landslide defeat by Lyndon Johnson.

The Movement's New Stage Brings New Problems

It is important to understand why a white backlash took place and would continue to grow up to the present day. Having basically secured the legal right to vote, blacks began to turn their attention to other substantive problems. They were determined to use their newly acquired political clout and the leverage gained by the civil rights movement's relationship with the Johnson administration to attack a host of economic and social problems.

The end of disfranchisement and segregation was an opportunity to address the acute needs of the African-American community. The civil rights progress of the decade following the 1954 *Brown* decision created rising expectations. Blacks anticipated a Second Reconstruction and accordingly redoubled their demand for government action against poverty and unemployment and for quality education, health care, and community-based economic development.

Civil rights progress would have a high price tag. Addressing long-unattended social ills was high on President Johnson's agenda. The centerpiece of his Great Society program, announced in his 1965 State of the Union address, was "an unconditional war on poverty." Within two years LBJ would put into place a new student loan program, Medicare, Medicaid, food stamps, Head Start, and establish the Office of Economic Opportunity. In 1967 he nominated the first African American to the Supreme

Court, Thurgood Marshall, who as the general counsel for the NAACP Legal Defense Fund had argued the *Brown v. Board of Education* case. Like Martin Luther King, and possibly influenced by his ongoing dialogue with King, Johnson anticipated what most whites did not, that the next stage of the struggle for racial justice would center on economic equality.

His speech at Howard University's commencement in 1965 indicated that President Johnson embraced an expansion of the mission of the civil rights movement. "We seek not just freedom," he said, "but opportunity . . . not just equality as a right and a theory but equality as a fact and as a result."[31] Johnson also recognized the need for government and society to take special steps, "affirmative action" as President Kennedy had called it, to facilitate blacks in overcoming a centuries-old legacy of discrimination and disadvantage.

> You do not take a person who for years has been hobbled by chains and liberate him, bring him up to the starting line of a race and then say, "You are free to compete with all the others," and still justly believe you have been completely fair.[32]

Many whites took these words as an implicit assault on white skin privilege. Those who had benefited directly or indirectly from racial discrimination in having a racial monopoly on many categories of employment, housing, and education were going to have to share. Not only in the South, but sometimes more intensely in the North, working-class and middle-class whites scurried to protect what many of them termed "our jobs," "our neighborhoods," and "our schools." Affirmative action would not be confined to the South; it would affect hiring and upgrading, job training, open housing, budget priorities, busing, and redlining by banks, real estate firms, and insurance companies.

The white backlash, particularly in the North, led politicians to play the "race card." Even though it was not good for the country, George Wallace's campaign proved that whipping up white resentment made for good politics. The more the Republicans found they could win with this approach, the more they used it.[33]

That the right wing of the Republican Party had appropriated Wallace's message while distancing itself from the man was evident in the 1968 presidential election. Richard Nixon adopted a "southern strategy" of appealing to whites with racist codewords like "law and order," "crime in the streets," "merit," and attacks on "tax and spend liberals." In a three-way race in which the Democrats were sharply divided over opposition to the war in Vietnam and George Wallace claimed just over 10 percent of the turnout, Nixon became president by winning only 43 percent of the vote. He quickly recast his minority support into a mandate from the "silent majority," to escalate the war in Vietnam as well as sanction an FBI-led campaign of harassment, destabilization, and disruption of the activities of black radicals, especially the Black Panther Party.

African-American Opposition to the Vietnam War

Opposition to the Vietnam War by growing segments of the black community; the sagging fortunes of the U.S. economy, which made it increasingly difficult to provide guns and butter; the radicalization of black rhetoric, including the advocacy of violence and racial separatism by some groups, the expanding white backlash against affirmative action and court-ordered busing; and Republican skill in playing the race card all acted to disrupt the unity of the democratic forces. These issues began to undermine the alliance between the civil rights movement and the Johnson administration, and to drive a wedge between black leaders and civil rights organizations. The spread of African-American opposition to the war in Vietnam was an especially sore point with President Johnson, who felt betrayed after all he had done for the cause of civil rights. SNCC had come out against the war. SNCC's position would exert tremendous influence not only on black young people, but also on large numbers of white youth. In a unique way, SNCC's antiwar posture intensified the radicalization of young activists.

Muhammad Ali, one of the most well-known and liked personalities in the world, refused induction into the armed forces and was stripped of his heavyweight boxing title. This, perhaps more than any other single event, crystallized the opposition of black youth.

Antiwar sentiment was also expressed in popular black music. Freda Payne sang, "Bring the Boys Home," while the Temptations crooned, "Stop the War!" Most of all, opposition to the war was propelled by the disproportionate number of casualties endured by African-American troops and the realization in the African-American community that blacks could not get at home the freedom that they were fighting for in Vietnam. In the minds of millions of African Americans, the struggle for civil rights merged with opposition to the war.

King also became more vocal in his opposition. While acknowledging Johnson's highly significant contributions to civil rights and voting rights, King believed that it was inconsistent politically to separate civil rights from the struggle for peace. Although he especially did not like the implication that a black could not judge foreign policy competently, his reasons for opposing Johnson's Vietnam policy were deeply moral and practical. The war was wrong on its merits and in its consequences.

> Then came the buildup in Vietnam and I watched the program [War on Poverty] broken and eviscerated as if it were some idle political plaything of a society gone mad on war, and I knew that America would never invest the necessary funds or energies in rehabilitation of its

poor so long as adventures like Vietnam continued to draw men and skills and money like some
demonic suction tube. So I was increasingly compelled to see the war as an enemy of the poor
and to attack it as such.[34]

"A Season of Suffering"

King had been prophetic at the end of the Selma to
Montgomery march in speaking of a "season of suffering."
It began the night Viola Liuzzo, a white Detroit housewife
and union activist who had come to Alabama to help on
logistics, was killed while driving marchers back to Selma.
It did not abate the next year when James Meredith was
shot and seriously wounded while staging a one-person
"Walk Against Fear" in Mississippi.

Suffering and violence continued through the "long,
hot summers" of 1966 and 1967, when "the fire next time"
that James Baldwin predicted exploded in Newark and
Detroit and dozens of other cities. It occurred in the rice
paddies, grassy plains, and "strategic hamlets" of Vietnam
as firefights, body counts, and carpet bombing increased.
A season of suffering persisted well into 1968, where on
the balcony of the Lorraine Motel in Memphis, Tennessee,
just past six in the evening of the fourth of April, an assas-
sin's bullet pierced the side of the head of Martin Luther
King, Jr. Minutes later, the "drum major of peace and justice" was dead.

King's assassination marked the demise of an era of
promise. The bullet that shattered his life also shattered
the nation's resolve and the African-American freedom
movement's moral compass. A young generation of dream-
ers became cynical. Something in the African-American
community itself perished. The white backlash now confronted a black backlash. Already before his death the
broad-based civil rights coalition he had helped to assemble had begun to unravel. After his death, the nonviolent,
multiracial coalition he represented was superseded by

the Black Power movement, which was taking on a separatist bent.

Already in 1965, within days of passage of the Voting
Rights Act, the Watts section of Los Angeles erupted in
the flames of rebellion. By the late 1960s, elements within SNCC and CORE claimed that whites had no role in
black organizations or the black community. The idea of
ghetto rebellions, rioting, and even armed struggle gained
in favor. Anger and alienation that was particularly strong
among black youth radicalized the tactics and rhetoric of
the Black Power movement that defied reality and sometimes rationality.[35]

Although it did not cause either the white backlash or
the fracturing of the civil rights coalition, the Black Power
movement did hasten them. The radicalism of the Black
Power movement, while often raising legitimate issues of
community control, also deepened political and ideological differences within the African-American movement.[36]

The black nationalist and Black Power radicals who
assumed the leadership of SNCC after 1966, particularly
Stokley Carmichael and H. Rap Brown, and the black cultural nationalist groups and the Black Panther Party pitted themselves against the NAACP, the Urban League,
and SCLC. The late Malcolm X, at least as the radical
nationalists understood him, became their role model—
one that they counterpoised to Martin Luther King.

The fracturing of black unity could not have come at
a worse time. Greater unity and broader alliances were
needed to transform the struggle for racial justice into a
war on poverty and to resist the Republican-led white
backlash. And in a remarkable contrast to the days when
civil rights protesters enjoyed extensive public sympathy
and support, the Black Power advocates reinforced white
fears, helped to accelerate white flight, and provoked some
white hostility.

The consequences of the decline of a multiracial coalition, deterioration of congressional support for further
civil rights progress, and the diversion of a substantial

segment of black sentiment and activism in the direction of go-it-along nationalism at the end of the 1960s would be catastrophic by the start of the 1980s. Instead of a war on poverty, the late 1960s and early 1970s brought a war on the poor, on radical black activists, and on the people of Southeast Asia. Despite the brief interlude of Democrat Jimmy Carter's presidency in the aftermath of the Watergate scandal and Nixon's resignation, the receding waters of the River of Freedom and dispersal of the civil rights coalition would give way to an era of right-wing Republicanism.

Within a decade the arch-conservative former governor of California, Ronald Reagan, would be elected president. The white backlash would then emanate from the White House, not from southern segregationists or northern white ethnic groups attempting to preserve racially exclusionary suburbs. The programs that Lyndon Johnson introduced, President Reagan and, following him, President George Bush, would eliminate or severely reduce. The legal, legislative, electoral, and material achievements of African Americans would be subjected to relentless assault—sometimes with quiet assent from growing numbers of Democrats.

"Keep on Pushing"

Today, when looking back nearly thirty years from whence the River of Freedom flowed in the fifties and sixties, it is possible to see how enormous the loss of King's leadership and the movement's focus has been, and how severe were the setbacks and defeats. In earlier periods, other leaders had fallen, and the African-American community had to endure disappointment, betrayal, and defeat. Events would soon show that other setbacks were to be sustained in the seventies, eighties, and mid-nineties. Navigating the River of Freedom is no easy task; it never has been and it never will be.

As long as the mighty waters of the River of Freedom flowed, the struggle for equality would continue—to the

155

next bend, and then passing it, to another inevitable rush of rapids. And mighty were its contributions not only to African-American progress, but also to other movements and to the expansion of democracy in America.

- Nonviolent resistance and the direct mass action of African Americans set an example for other racial minorities, activists against the Vietnam War, and feminists. They too adopted tactics involving sit-ins, boycotts, demonstrations, and marches on Washington.
- The African-American movement taught others the potential for expanding the limits of democracy, for utilizing the constitutional responsibilities of the executive, legislative, and judicial branches to enforce equal rights.
- The legislative victories of African Americans from the Reconstruction Act of 1866, through the Fourteenth and Fifteenth amendments, to the Civil Rights Act of 1964 and the Voting Rights Act of 1965 paved the way for other minorities, women, the elderly, the disabled, and lesbians and gays to end discrimination and gain political representation.
- African Americans enriched American democracy with concepts of due process and equality before the law, they forced the country to grapple with the issues of the rights of racial minorities, to protect the rights of the accused, and to safeguard the right to dissent; they helped pioneer the doctrine of "one person, one vote," thus enlarging representative democracy.

In the 1960s the Student Nonviolent Coordinating Committee united young people across lines of race, class, and gender. SNCC activists went on to champion political participation in the Black Belt, and free speech on the college campuses, and to build a peace majority in opposition to the war in Vietnam.

From slave revolts to the Underground Railroad to

the civil rights movement to the present, African-American women have been in the forefront of the struggle. Not infrequently, black women have had to confront attitudes of male supremacy as well as racism. In many ways it was the perseverance of African-American women in their roles as leaders, strategists, organizers, educators, and activists that helped make victory possible. The civil rights movement was particularly notable for the leadership given it by women; for example, Rosa Parks, Ella Baker, Septima Clarke, Fannie Lou Hamer, Diane Nash, Ruby Doris Robinson, Bernice Reagon Johnson (now of Sweet Honey in the Rock), Eleanor Holmes Norton (who now represents the District of Columbia in the House of Representatives), and Marian Wright Edelman (founder and president of the Children's Defense Fund).

By the same measure, as Clayborne Carson notes, "Just as the origins of the nineteenth-century women's rights movement can be traced to the involvement of women in the abolitionist struggle, so the modern [feminist] movement received an important impetus from SNCC and the civil rights struggle of the 1960s."[37] In fact, a workshop on the role of women at a SNCC staff retreat produced one of the first theoretical documents on sexism within the civil rights movement.[38]

The Struggle Continues

In the early 1960s a group called the Impressions recorded a tune, "Keep On Pushing," written by its lead singer, Curtis Mayfield, which has the following line: "We can't stop now. We've just got to keep on pushing." And so it was. The African-American struggle would "keep on pushing" against new obstacles, on to new challenges, for more far-reaching democratic demands: affirmative action, economic equality, political empowerment, environmental justice.

SOURCE NOTES

CHAPTER 1

1. John Hope Franklin, *From Slavery to Freedom: A History of Negro Americans* (New York: Vintage Books, third edition, 1969), 127–28.
2. Ibid., 128–29.
3. Ibid., 129.
4. Sethard Fisher, *From Margin to Mainstream: The Social Progress of Black Americans* (Boston: Rowman & Littlefield Publishers, second edition, 1992), 14.
5. Ibid., 130.
6. Benjamin Quarles, *The Negro in the Making of America* (New York: Collier Books, 1964), 46–50.
7. Lerone Bennett, Jr., *Before the Mayflower: A History of Black America 1619–1964* (Baltimore: Penguin Books, revised edition, 1966), 52–59.
8. Ibid., 62.

CHAPTER 2

1. Eli Ginsberg and Alfred S. Eichner, *The Troublesome Presence: Democracy and Black Americans* (New Brunswick, N.J.: Transaction Publishers, 1993), 50–51.
2. Quoted in Ginsberg and Eichner, 53.

CHAPTER 3

1. Herbert Aptheker, *Early Years of the Republic: From the End of the Revolution to the First Administration of Washington 1783–1793* (New York: International Publishers, 1976), 127.
2. Ibid., 128.
3. Ibid., 127.
4. John Hope Franklin, *From Slavery to Freedom: A History of Negro Americans* (New York: Vintage Books, 1969), 147.
5. Quoted in Ginsberg and Eichner, 90.
6. Ibid., 88.
7. Ibid., 88.
8. Ibid., 91.
9. Franklin, 185–86.
10. Ibid., 186.
11. Ibid., 187.
12. Ibid., 267–68.
13. Ibid., 268.

CHAPTER 4

1. John Hope Franklin, *From Slavery to Freedom: A History of Negro Americans*, 162–63.
2. C. Eric Lincoln and Lawrence H. Mamiya, *The Black Church in the African American Experience* (Durham: Duke University Press, 1990), 52.
3. Ibid., 8.
4. Ibid., 25.
5. William F. Cheek, *Black Resistance Before the Civil War* (Beverly Hills, Calif.: Glencoe Press, 1970), 27.
6. Franklin, 259–60.
7. Ibid., 258.
8. Quoted in Franklin, *From Slavery to Freedom*, 211.
9. Bennett, 114.
10. Ibid., 116.
11. 212–213; also see: Cheek, *Black Resistance*, 22–25.

CHAPTER 5

1. Philip S. Foner, *ed., The Life and Writings of Frederick Douglass*, 4 vols. (New York: International Publishers, 1970), vol. 3, 23.
2. Ibid., 56.
3. Ibid., 178–82.
4. Ibid., 178.
5. Eileen Shields–West, *The World Almanac of Presidential Campaigns* (New York: Pharos Books, 1992), 80.
6. Philip S. Foner, ed., vol. 2, 67, 70, 71.
7. Philip S. Foner, ed., *Douglass,* vol. 2, 367, 369.
8. Ibid.
9. Ibid., 83.
10. Philip S. Foner, vol. 3, 72.
11. Ibid., 98.
12. Ibid., 98.
13. Ibid., 85.
14. Charles A. Beard and Mary R. Beard, *A Basic History of the United States* (Philadelphia: Garden City Publishers, 1944), 266–69.
15. Philip S. Foner, vol. 3, 13.
16. Ibid., 13.

CHAPTER 6

1. Lerone Bennett, Jr., *Before the Mayflower,* 191.
2. Philip S. Foner, *Frederick Douglass,* vol. 3, 17.
3. Charles A. Beard and Mary Beard, *A Basic History of the United States,* 278–79.
4. Franklin, *From Slavery to Freedom,* 281.
5. Ibid., 25.
6. *The New York Public Library Desk Reference* (New York: Stonesong Press Book, 1989), 718.
7. Quoted in Quarles, *The Negro in the Making of America,* 119.
8. Bennett, *Before the Mayflower, 190–91.*
9. Ibid., 206.
10. Ibid., 189.

11. See: Franklin, 290–94; Quarles, 118–22; and Bennett, 205.
12. Bennett, 207.
13. Richard Hofstadter, ed., *Great Issues in American History: From the Revolution to the Civil War, 1765–1865* (New York: Vintage Books, 1958), vol.II, 414–15.
14. Franklin, 302.
15. Franklin, 301.

CHAPTER 7

1. Eric Foner, *Reconstruction: America's Unfinished Business* (New York: Harper and Row, 1988),180.
2. Quoted in Bennett, *Before the Mayflower,* 193.
3. Eric Foner, 199.
4. Philip S. Foner, *Frederick Douglass,* vol. 3, 16.
5. Ginsberg and Eichner, *The Troublesome Presence,* 133–34.
6. Ibid., 134.
7. Philip S. Foner, vol. 3, 23.
8. Ibid., 30.

CHAPTER 8

1. W.E.B. DuBois, *Black Reconstruction in America 1860–1880* (Cleveland: Meridan Books, first printing, 1964, originally published in 1935), 372.
2. Quoted in Eric Foner, *Reconstruction,* 4.
3. DuBois, *Black Reconstruction,* 320.
4. Quoted in Eric Foner, 288.
5. Eric Foner, 288.
6. Lerone Bennett, Jr., *Black Power USA,* 104.
7. Ibid., 140.
8. Bennett, *Before the Mayflower,* 236.
9. The title of a song made famous by Billie Holiday. "Strange Fruit" is a reference to lynching.

CHAPTER 9

1. Bennett, *Black Power USA,* 407.
2. Ibid., 412–13.

3. Quoted in Ginsberg and Eichner, *The Troublesome Presence*, 185.

4. Ibid, 415.

5. Quoted in Bennett, *Black Power USA,* 410.

6. Ginsberg and Eischner, 186.

7. Chandler Davidson, *ed., Minority Vote Dilution* (Washington, D.C.: Howard University Press, 1989), 30–37.

8. Woodward, *The Strange Career of Jim Crow*, 85.

9. Harvard Sitkoff, *A New Deal for Blacks: The Emergence of Civil Rights as a National Issue* (New York: Oxford University Press, 1981), 8.

10. Bennett, *Before the Mayflower*, 232.

11. Bennett, *Before the Mayflower*, 268.

CHAPTER 10

1. Philip S. Foner, *Frederick Douglass*, vol.4, 511.

2. Robert L. Factor, *The Black Response to America: Men, Ideals and Organization from Frederick Douglass to the NAACP* (Reading, Mass.: Addison–Wesley, 1970), 168, 171.

3. Herbert Aptheker, *A Documentary History of the Negro People in the United States: From the Reconstruction Era to 1910* (New York: Citadel Press, fourth edition, 1968), 755.

4. Robert H. Brisbane, *The Black Vanguard: Origins of the Negro Social Revolution 1900–1960* (Valley Forge, Pa: Judson Press, second printing, 1970), 29–30.

5. Brisbane, 30.

6. Quoted in Factor, 261.

7. W.E.B. Dubois, *The Souls of Black Folk* in *Three Negro Classics* (New York: Avon Books, 1965), 265.

8. Ibid., 254.

9. Bennett, *Before the Mayflower*, 336.

CHAPTER 11

1. William H. Harris, *The Harder We Run: Black Workers Since the Civil War* (New York: Oxford University Press, 1982), 55–56.

2. Ibid., 272.
3. Phillip S. Foner, *Organized Labor and the Black Worker 1619–1973* (New York: Praeger Publishers, 1974), 272. Also see: Harvard Sitkoff, *A New Deal for Blacks: The Emergence of Civil Rights as a National Issue, Volume I: The Depression Decade* (New York: Oxford University Press, 1981), 31.
4. Philip Foner, 190.
5. Ibid., 189.
6. Harvard Sitkoff, *The Struggle for Black Equality 1954–1980* (New York: Hill and Wang, 1989), 36–37, 39.
7. Ibid., 39–41.
8. James Steele, *Organized Labor and the Development of Civil Rights Policy* (unpublished, Empire State College Graduate Program, December 16, 1991), 22.
9. Sitkoff, *A New Deal for Blacks,* 48.
10. Sitkoff, 88–90.
11. Franklin, *From Slavery to Freedom,* 533, 536, 538.
12. Ibid., 532.
13. Robert H. Zeigler, *American Workers, American Unions, 1920–1985* (Baltimore: The Johns Hopkins University Press, 1986), 26.
14. Philip S. Foner, *Organized Labor,* 215.
15. Zeigler, *American Workers, American Unions*, 51–52.
16. Philip S. Foner, *Organized Labor,* 231.
17. Franklin, 544–45.
18. Andrew J. Taylor, *Trade Unions and Politics: A Comparative Introduction* (New York: St. Martin's Press, 1989), 7–8.
19. Harvard Sitkoff, *The Struggle for Black Equality 1954–1980*, 10.
20. Hugh David Graham, *The Civil Rights Era: Origins and Development of National Policy* (New York: Oxford University Press, 1990), 20–21.
21. Hanes Walton, Jr., *When the Marching Stopped: The Politics of Civil Rights Regulatory Agencies (Albany, NY: The State University of New York Press, 1988),* 7.

22. Graham, 10.
23. Ibid., 11.

CHAPTER 12

1. Manning Marable, *Race, Reform and Rebellion: The Second Reconstruction in Black America, 1945–1982* (Jackson, Miss.: University of Mississippi Press, 4th printing, 1989), 25–26.
2. Gerald Horne, *Black and Red: W.E.B. Dubois and the Afro-American Response to the Cold War 1944–1963* (Albany: State University of New York Press, 1986), 151. Also see: chapter 14.
3. Clayborne Carson, *In Struggle: SNCC and the Black Awakening of the 1960s* (Cambridge, Mass.: Harvard University Press, 1981), 15.
4. Robert H. Brisbane, *The Black Vanguard*, 191–96.
5. Harvard Sitkoff, *The Struggle for Black Equality 1954–1980*, 11.
6. Richard Kluger, *Simple Justice: The History of Brown v. Board of Education and Black America's Struggle for Equality* (New York: Vintage Books, 1977), 665.
7. Ibid., 678–99.
8. See: Marable, *Race, Reform and Rebellion*.
9. Taylor Branch, *Parting the Waters: America in the King Years 1954–63* (New York: Simon and Schuster, 1988), 145–46, 158–59, 167, 188, 193–96.
10. Martin Luther King, Jr., *Stride Toward Freedom: The Montgomery Story* (New York: Harper & Row, 1964, First Perennial Library edition), 78–79. The reader will find it interesting to read Chapter VI "Pilgrimage to Nonviolence" in its entirety.
11. Ibid., 79.
12. Branch, *Parting the Waters*, 140.
13. Taken from transcript of "Eyes on the Prize" segment.
14. Kluger, 754; Sitkoff, *Black Equality*, 36.
15. David Garrow, *Bearing the Cross: Martin Luther King, Jr., and the Southern Christian Leadership Conference* (New York: William Morrow and Company, 1986), 83–90.

16. Carson, *In Struggle*, 9–12.
17. Ibid., 19–20.
18. Branch, 656–672.
19. Martin Luther King, Jr., *Why We Can't Wait* (New York: New American Library, 1964, 5th printing), 76–96.
20. Ibid, 76.
21. Branch, 807.
22. Ibid., 825.
23. Sitkoff, 151–52.
24. Ibid., 153.
25. Manning Marable, *Black American Politics: From the Washington Marches to Jesse Jackson* (London: Verso, 1983), 91.
26. Quoted in *Beyond the Color Line* (program book for the 125th Anniversary Tribute to W.E.B. DuBois), New York City, October 4, 1993.
27. Carson, 93.
28. Marable, *Black American Politics*, 95.
29. Martin Luther King, Jr., "I Have A Dream," in August Meier, Elliott Rudwick, and Francis L. Broderwick, *Black Protest Thought in the Twentieth Century* (New York: Bobbs-Merrill Company, 1971, second edition), 348.

CHAPTER 13

1. Mark Stern, *Calculating visions: Kennedy, Johnson and Civil Rights* (New Brunswick, NJ: Rutgers University Press, 1992), 134, 145, 148.
2. Ibid., 161, 162.
3. Ibid., 160–61.
4. Ibid., 168–72, 173–76, 182–84.
5. Ibid., 183–84.
6. Thomas R. Dye, *The Politics of Equality* (New York: Bobbs-Merrill, 1971), 57.
7. Ibid., 57–58.
8. Ibid., 58.
9. Stern, 204–209.
10. Ibid., 210.

11. Ibid., 211.
12. Jaynes and Williams, *A Common Destiny*, 233, 235; Thomas E. Cavanagh, *The Impact of the Black Electorate* (Joint Center for Political Studies: Washington, D.C., 1984), 17.
13. Jaynes and Williams, 233; Ronald W. Walters, *Black Presidential Politics in America: A Strategic Approach* (State University of New York Press: Albany, NY, 1988), 38.
14. Quoted in Sitkoff, *The Struggle for Black Equality*, 63–64.
15. Steven F. Lawson, *Black Ballots: Voting Rights in the South, 1944–1969* (New York: Columbia University Press, 1976), 308–309.
16. Ibid., 307–308.
17. Ibid., 309.
18. Ibid., 410.
19. Leon Friedman, ed., *The Civil Rights Reader: Basic Document of the Civil Rights Movement* (New York: Walker and Company, revised edition, 1968), 260.
20. Ibid., 263.
21. Ibid., 264.
22. Ibid., 265.
23. Juan Williams, *Eyes On the Prize: America's Civil Rights Years, 1954–1965* (New York: Viking Penguin, 1987), 283.
24. James M. Washington, ed., *A Testament of Hope: The Essential Writings and Speeches of Martin Luther King, Jr.* (New York: Harper Collins, 1991), 230.
25. Stern, 227–28.
26. Dye, 55.
27. U.S. Commission on Civil Rights, *The Voting Rights Act: Unfulfilled Goals* (Washington: U.S. Commission on Civil Rights, 1981), 4–5.
28. Jaynes and Williams, *A Common Destiny*, 232–38.
29. Lawson, *Black Ballots*, 329.
30. Ibid., 334.
31. Graham, Hugh Davis, *The Civil Rights Era: Origins*

and Development of National Policy (New York: Oxford University Press, 1990), 174.

32. Ibid., 174.

33. See: Thomas Byrne Edsall and Mary D. Edsall, *Chain Reaction: The Impact of Race, Rights, and Taxes on American Politics* (New York: W.W. Norton, 1991), chapters 3 and 4.

34. King, *Essential Writings and Speeches*, 232–33.

35. See Clayborne Carson, *In struggle*, chapters 14 and 14.

36. Robert Weisbrot, *Freedom Bound: A History of America's Civil Rights Movement* (New York: W.W. Norton, 1990), 204–216.

37. Carson, 147.

38. Ibid.

FOR FURTHER READING

Bennett, Lerone, Jr. *Before the Mayflower: A History of Black America, 1464–1619.* Baltimore: Penguin Books, 1966.

DuBois, W. E. B. *Black Reconstruction in America, 1860–1880.* Cleveland: Meridan Books, 1964, originally published in 1935.

DuBois, W. E. B. *The Souls of Black Folk.* In *Three Negro Classics.* New York: Avon Books, 1965.

Factor, Robert L. *The Black Response to America: Men, Ideals, and Organization from Frederick Douglass to the NAACP.* Reading, Mass.: Addison-Wesley Publishing Co., 1970.

Foner, Philip S. *The Life and Writings of Frederick Douglass.* 4 vols. New York: International Publishers, 1970.

Foner, Philip S. *Organized Labor and the Black Worker, 1619–1973.* New York: Praeger Publishers, 1974.

Ginsberg, Eli, and Alfred S. Eichner. *The Troublesome Presence: Democracy and Black Americans.* New Brunswick, N.J.: Transaction Publishers, 1993.

Franklin, John Hope. *From Slavery to Freedom: A History of Negro Americans.* 3rd ed. New York: Vintage Books, 1969.

Garrow, David. *Bearing the Cross: Martin Luther King, Jr., and the Southern Christian Leadership Conference.* New York: William Morrow and Company, 1986.

King, Martin Luther, Jr. *Stride Toward Freedom: The Montgomery Story.* New York: Harper and Row, 1964.

King, Martin Luther, Jr. *Why We Can't Wait.* 5th printing. New York: New American Library, 1964.

Lincoln, C. Eric, and Lawrence H. Mamiya. *The Black Church in the African American Experience.* Durham, N.C.: Duke University Press, 1990

Marable, Manning. *Race, Reform and Rebellion: The Second Reconstruction in Black America, 1945–1982.* 4th printing. Jackson, Miss.: University of Mississippi Press, 1989.

Quarles, Benjamin. *The Negro in the Making of America.* New York: Collier Books, 1964.

Sitkoff, Harvard. *The Struggle for Black Equality, 1954–1980.* New York: Hill and Wang, 1989.

Washington, James M., ed. *A Testament of Hope: The Essential Writings and Speeches of Martin Luther King, Jr.* New York: HarperCollins, 1991.

Williams, Juan. *Eyes on the Prize: America's Civil Rights Years, 1954–1965.* New York: Viking Penguin, 1987.

INDEX

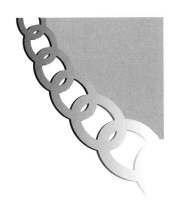

ABOUT THE AUTHOR

James Steele is an activist and the head of Breakthrough Political Consultants. He has participated in the Civil Rights Movement, has worked in the electoral campaigns of Jesse Jackson, and has been a consultant to the New York City mayoral campaigns of David Dinkins. He and his wife, a school principal, live with their children in Brooklyn, New York.